# STRATEGIC STUDIES INSTITUTE

The Strategic Studies Institute (SSI) is part of the U.S. Army War College and is the strategic-level study agent for issues related to national security and military strategy with emphasis on geostrategic analysis.

The mission of SSI is to use independent analysis to conduct strategic studies that develop policy recommendations on:

- Strategy, planning, and policy for joint and combined employment of military forces;

- Regional strategic appraisals;

- The nature of land warfare;

- Matters affecting the Army's future;

- The concepts, philosophy, and theory of strategy; and,

- Other issues of importance to the leadership of the Army.

Studies produced by civilian and military analysts concern topics having strategic implications for the Army, the Department of Defense, and the larger national security community.

In addition to its studies, SSI publishes special reports on topics of special or immediate interest. These include edited proceedings of conferences and topically oriented roundtables, expanded trip reports, and quick-reaction responses to senior Army leaders.

The Institute provides a valuable analytical capability within the Army to address strategic and other issues in support of Army participation in national security policy formulation.

Strategic Studies Institute
and
U.S. Army War College Press

# THE STRATEGIC LESSONS UNLEARNED FROM VIETNAM, IRAQ, AND AFGHANISTAN:

## Why the Afghan National Security Forces Will Not Hold, and the Implications for the U.S. Army in Afghanistan

M. Chris Mason

June 2015

*****

*****

Comments pertaining to this report are invited and should be forwarded to: Director, Strategic Studies Institute and U.S. Army War College Press, U.S. Army War College, 47 Ashburn Drive, Carlisle, PA 17013-5010.

*****

All Strategic Studies Institute (SSI) and U.S. Army War College (USAWC) Press publications may be downloaded free of charge from the SSI website. Hard copies of this report may also be obtained free of charge while supplies last by placing an order on the SSI website. SSI publications may be quoted or reprinted in part or in full with permission and appropriate credit given to the U.S. Army Strategic Studies Institute and U.S. Army War College Press, U.S. Army War College, Carlisle, PA. Contact SSI by visiting our website at the following address: *www.StrategicStudiesInstitute.army.mil.*

*****

The Strategic Studies Institute and U.S. Army War College Press publishes a monthly email newsletter to update the national security community on the research of our analysts, recent and forthcoming publications, and upcoming conferences sponsored by the Institute. Each newsletter also provides a strategic commentary by one of our research analysts. If you are interested in receiving this newsletter, please subscribe on the SSI website at *www.StrategicStudiesInstitute.army.mil/newsletter.*

ISBN 1-58487-683-2

# CONTENTS

# FOREWORD

Military personnel who have experience in Afghanistan, Iraq, or Vietnam, as well as senior leaders and military historians alike, will find this book by Dr. Chris Mason thought-provoking and useful. Dr. Mason examines indigenous personnel issues at the tactical, operational, and strategic levels of war and uses empirical data and exhaustive research to argue that all three wars were lost before the first shots were fired—not on the battlefield, but at the strategic level of war.

The United States interpreted all three conflicts as insurgencies, Mason writes, when in fact all three were civil wars in which the United States took a side. Success was never possible from the outset, his provocative thesis argues, because none of the three countries were nations for which the majority of their citizens were willing to fight and die. Nation-building is a slow, evolutionary, internal process through which the political identity of the peoples within a country's borders matures over centuries to transcend tribalism, secularism, and ethnic divides, Mason argues, until it reaches a pervasive sense of nationhood. "Nation-building," and democracy-importation on the point of foreign bayonets, this book maintains, is impossible.

Throughout this book, Mason continually examines the issues from new perspectives and introduces new tactical, operational, and strategic paradigms. His explication in Part II of what will happen in Afghanistan year-by-year from 2015 to 2019 unless major changes occur in theater is bold, captivating, stark—and credible. The contributions to operational wargaming in Afghanistan in Appendix II alone make this publication a must-read. His comparative statistical and qualitative analyses of the Afghan National Security Forces today, and those in Vietnam and Iraq at their respective points of collapse, are no less eye-opening and thought provoking. His examination of the bureaucratic and psychological obstacles to policymaking and objective strategic analysis in Part III should be absorbed by every military officer in the United States.

In short, this is a provocative, highly readable, and wide-ranging analysis of the future of Afghanistan and the future of land warfare. Not everyone will like or agree with his conclusions, but they are a valuable contribution to understanding the conflicts in Vietnam, Iraq, and Afghanistan—and those the U.S. Army may fight in the future—in an important new way.

DOUGLAS C. LOVELACE, JR.
Director
Strategic Studies Institute and
    U.S. Army War College Press

# ABOUT THE AUTHOR

M. CHRIS MASON joined the faculty at the Strategic Studies Institute as a Professor of National Security Affairs in June 2014. He has worked in and on Afghanistan for the past 15 years. Dr. Mason retired from the Foreign Service in 2005 and worked as the South Asia desk officer for the Marine Corps' Center for Advanced Operational Culture and Language for several years, where he wrote the Marine Corps deployer's guide to Afghan culture and the guide to Operational Pashtunwali. He has deployed to and traveled to Afghanistan and Pakistan numerous times, beginning in December 2001, serving as the political officer on the Provincial Reconstruction Team in Paktika in 2005. Dr. Mason authored the first paper in the U.S. Government on the Afghan National Army (ANA) in October 2001, and worked for 5 years on ANA, Afghan National Police and other security issues as the representative of the Bureau of Political Military Affairs to the Afghan Interagency Operations Group. From 1981 to 1986, he served as a regular U.S. Navy Officer on active duty, including tours as the Gunnery Officer on the USS *John Young* (DD973) and a Naval Gunfire Liaison Officer with 2d Battalion 12th Marines in Okinawa, Japan, and 2d Air Naval Gunfire Liaison Company (ANGLICO [Airborne]) at Camp Lejeune, North Carolina. Dr. Mason was a Peace Corps Volunteer in rural development in South America from 1977 to 1979. Dr. Mason trained tens of thousands of deploying American and North Atlantic Treaty Organization military personnel on military and cultural aspects of the war in Afghanistan, and has published widely on Afghanistan and Pakistan in numerous publications over the past 10 years. Dr. Mason holds a bachelor's degree with Honors from Carnegie Mellon University; graduated with Distinction from the resident Command and General Staff College course at the Marine Corps University, Quantico, VA; holds a masters degree in military studies from the Marine Corps University, and a Ph.D. in military and Central Asian history from The George Washington University, Washington, DC.

# INTRODUCTION

Those who cannot remember the past are condemned to repeat it.

George Santayana[1]

Anyone wanting to commit American ground forces to the mainland of Asia should have his head examined.

Douglas MacArthur, 1961[2]

Any future defense secretary who advises the president to again send a big American land army into Asia or into the Middle East or Africa should have his head examined.

Secretary of Defense Robert Gates, 2011[3]

The wars in Vietnam, Iraq, and Afghanistan were all fought after General Douglas MacArthur's admonition in 1961 to President John Kennedy not to commit land forces to a war in Asia. Three times in 40 years, the United States committed large numbers of U.S. ground forces to land wars in Asia anyway and lost all three of them, not on the battlefield, but at the strategic level of war. As of December 2014, 65,069 Americans have died in those wars. So far, no one has had their head examined. This book seeks to conduct that examination on a national strategic level, and to lay out for senior military leaders the explicit lessons of Vietnam, Iraq, and Afghanistan that remain unlearned and which would have prevented every single one of those deaths.

1

This book is written in three parts. It builds from the tactical to the operational to the strategic level of war. The purpose of Part I is to explain why the security forces of Afghanistan cannot hold back the Taliban in the southern half of the country based on analysis using comparisons with the military and political situations at the time of the U.S. withdrawals from Vietnam and Iraq. Part II will examine, at the operational level of war, what will happen in Afghanistan year-by-year over the next 5 years (from 2015 to 2019), the concept of "nation-building," and the resulting operational lessons from the wars in Vietnam, Iraq, and Afghanistan. Part III synthesizes Parts I and II, examines obstacles to strategic judgment when faced with this kind of information, and provides a strategic guide for evaluating all international military engagements from the point of view of land warfare. These strategic lessons from Vietnam, Iraq, and Afghanistan should form the foundation of consideration and strategic thought for all future potential land warfare.

From the American perspective, all three conflicts were counterinsurgencies, but this is not a book about counterinsurgency, or to what extent the future Army should train and be equipped for counterinsurgency, or even if counterinsurgency doctrine itself is sound. Counterinsurgency works if the people living inside the insurgency want it to work, and it fails if they do not. Foreigners can build architecture, but they cannot build a nation. Extensive empirical data shows conclusively that there was no increase in local community support for the Afghan government, for example, after the delivery of schools, roads, clinics, and so on, by the counterinsurgents.[4] We built it, and they did not come. Furthermore, this data was available **before** the tactic of "clear, hold, and build" was widely implemented at enormous cost in blood and treasure.

The intent of this book is not to criticize at any level the military participants in these conflicts. With rare exceptions, the U.S. military fought honorably and capably in all three conflicts and achieved outcomes in each case that were, in grand strategic terms, about the best that could have been achieved. No disrespect to the men and women who went overseas and did the best jobs they could in complex environments under difficult conditions should be inferred in the pages that follow. There are no counterhistorical arguments about how these conflicts might have been better conducted with different tactics, operations, and strategies, if indeed there were any strategies, or any hypothetical alternative outcomes.

There are also neither impracticable "recommendations" for how to fix Afghanistan with the vague, and grandiose "musts" and "shoulds" that usually accompany analyses of this type, nor any trivial rearranging of deck chairs such as twiddling on the margins of force size and so on. Americans are a practical people restlessly in search of solutions, but some problems have no solutions, and Afghanistan is one of them. There are no silver bullets, and anything that could help salvage the situation is politically impossible. American officers are trained to find a way to win, but sometimes forces beyond the battlefield make negative outcomes inevitable. Instead, the intent of this book is to break up the ice of conventional thinking, which has calcified the discussion of these issues into such predictable patterns, and to demonstrate that the outcomes in Vietnam, Iraq, and Afghanistan were, in fact, predetermined by immutable political and cultural imperatives before the first shots were fired. This book will show that these tragedies were avoidable, and will define these immutable political and cultural

3

imperatives as strategic litmus tests for the security policy apparatus of the United States. They are especially critical to the Joint Chiefs of Staff as part of their processes for determining when, where, and how to engage U.S. military power.

## ENDNOTES - INTRODUCTION

1. George Santayana, "The Life of Reason, or the Phases of Human Progress," Vol. I, *Reason in Common Sense*, New York: Charles Scribner's Sons, 1920, p. 284.

2. James Douglass, *JFK and the Unspeakable: Why He Died and Why It Matters*, New York: Simon and Schuster, 2008, p. 102.

3. "Gates's Warning: Avoid Land War in Asia, Middle East, and Africa," *The Christian Science Monitor*, February 26, 2011, available from *www.csmonitor.com/USA/Military/2011/0226/Gates-s-warning-Avoid-land-war-in-Asia-Middle-East-and-Africa*.

4. Dr. Jennifer Brick, "The Political Economy of Customary Village Organizations in Rural Afghanistan," Madison, WI: University of Wisconsin-Madison, 2008.

# PART I:

# WHY THE AFGHAN NATIONAL SECURITY FORCES CANNOT HOLD, AND THE IMPLICATIONS FOR THE U.S. ARMY IN AFGHANISTAN

## SUMMARY

> All truth passes through three stages. First, it is ridiculed. Second, it is violently opposed. Third, it is accepted as being self-evident.
>
> Arthur Schopenhauer[1]

A new paper, article, or book seemingly appears almost daily about the future of Afghanistan, generally ruminating on "ifs" and "unknowns" before concluding that the outcome remains "uncertain." In fact, the outcome in Afghanistan and the events of the next 5 years are not difficult to foresee, and there is not really any realistic doubt about this outcome. Everything else is whistling past the strategic graveyard and magical thinking.[2] The conclusions drawn here are entirely in accord with the consensus of the U.S. intelligence community, as set out in the unclassified portions of a series of National Intelligence Estimates (NIEs) released to the public.[3] Indeed, this book is derived entirely from unclassified and publicly available documents and information sources, together with the author's interviews and conversations in unclassified public fora. Readers should bear in mind that the most pessimistic and negative information, such as district-by-district intelligence assessments of Taliban control in Afghanistan, are classified, and this book contains only information from the **more optimistic** sphere of public information. Nevertheless, some military readers of this book may still experience cognitive dissonance, so deeply has the ethos of optimism been ingrained in the culture of the military.

This is most often visible in the friction between the intelligence community and the military. The track record of intelligence assessments on Afghanistan being condemned by senior military leaders as being "too pessimistic," only to be proven to have been too **optimistic**, is a long one, but it has not changed the pattern.[4] In the past, Central Command (CENTCOM) leaders even went to the extraordinary step of demanding a **military** rebuttal to the pessimistic conclusions of Afghanistan NIEs.[5] The overall pattern for almost a decade has been that the intelligence community creates an NIE, the NIE is condemned by the military (which does not have a statutory role outside of the Defense Intelligence Agency in intelligence production and coordination), and the assessment proves to have been correct (or even understated).[6] When the next NIE is produced, the process is repeated. Nor is this new. The exact same thing happened during the Vietnam War. Indeed, this is just another of the extraordinary number of parallels between the wars in Afghanistan and Vietnam.[7] Sociologists and psychologists refer to this as the "backfire effect," or in clinical terms, the confirmation bias,[8] which is the odd but human tendency to interpret contradictory new evidence as confirmation of one's existing beliefs rather than as a reason to change them. Part III of this book will briefly examine the confirmation bias, why the U.S. military establishment is so frequently at odds with the intelligence community, and why there remains a disturbing tendency to downplay the consensus of our best intelligence analysts in favor of more optimistic military projections of capabilities and future events to the overall detriment of national security policy.

Regarding the future of Afghanistan, in blunt terms, the United States has been down this road at the strategic level twice before, in Vietnam and Iraq, and there is no viable rationale for why the results will be any different in Afghanistan. South Vietnam, Iraq, and Afghanistan are, or were, very different countries. Yet, at the strategic level of war, all three have critical commonalities, and these yield strategic lessons that remain unlearned. First and foremost, all three countries were artificial colonial relics with no pervasive sense of national identity. South Vietnam was the bastard stepchild of colonial French Indochina, the result of an inept post-war French effort to regain its colonies in Southeast Asia with ill-considered and ill-advised U.S. financial and logistical support.[9] Afghanistan was an unruly outlier of many empires when Central Asia was the heart of the world and cursed to be, in historian Arnold Toynbee's words, "the Eastern crossroads of history."[10] Its present cartographic form results from the desire to create a buffer of wilderness between the 18th and 19th century Russian and British empires.[11] Whether this 19th century European construct should be preserved at the cost of thousands of lives simply for the sake of preserving it goes unasked.

Iraq is another colonial relic (or was, as there seems little realistic possibility of it being reestablished de facto within its 1922/2005 de jure boundaries), concocted in a British imperial "absence of mind."[12] Its borders were randomly drawn in straight lines across the old Ottoman Empire by Gertrude Bell in 1918 and affirmed by the Treaty of Mohammara in 1922.[13] Indeed, imperial mapmakers like Bell created such lines all over Africa, the Middle East, and South Asia largely along geographical features or simply with a straight edge, with little regard for religious, tribal, linguistic, or ethnic realities on the ground. Slowly, these imperial maps are being redrawn from within, in places like Bangladesh, Sudan, Eritrea, East Timor, the former Yugoslavia, and Iraq, accompanied by bloodshed and stubbornly resisted as long as possible as a matter of principle by diplomats of the status quo at the United Nations (UN) and the State Department. The questions of whether places like Iraq, Syria, and Pakistan are actually ever going to be viable as nations at all, and should even **be** single countries are never asked when discussions of using military force arise. For whatever reason, foreign policy, and therefore military policy, always proceeds from the unquestioned assumption that failed and failing countries should be kept together as countries at all costs, even though unsustainable and unworkable borders usually lie at the core of their failure.

Second, all three conflicts were civil wars. This is another startling commonality of the wars in Vietnam, Iraq, and Afghanistan. In words that echo of Iraq and Afghanistan, Vietnam historian Jeffrey Record notes:

> By refusing to recognize or admit that the Vietnam War was from its inception primarily a civil war, and not part of a larger, centrally-directed international conspiracy, policymakers assumed that North Vietnam was, like the United States, waging a limited war, and therefore that it would be prepared to settle for something less than total victory (especially if confronted by military stalemate on the ground in the South and the threat of aerial bombardment of the North). In so making this assumption, policymakers not only ignored two millennia of Vietnamese history, but also excused themselves from confronting the harsh truth that civil wars are, for their indigenous

8

participants, total wars, and that no foreign participant in someone else's civil war can possibly have as great a stake in the conflict's outcome — and attendant willingness to sacrifice — as do the indigenous parties involved.[14]

Of the three countries under consideration in this book, South Vietnam came the closest to having a workable ethnic majority, but religious and socioeconomic divides created insurmountable obstacles to national unity, and ultimately to a meaningful sense of nationhood. None of three had ever been a democracy or came close to developing the social values that underpin western democracy. In each case, the United States attempted to impose one anyway. In each one, the U.S. Army (primarily) attempted to create a standing army in the exact model of the U.S. Army itself, which would be responsible for maintaining in power a U.S.-created system of government. All three of these governments were proclaimed "legitimate" based on the trappings of elections, despite elections having never been a source of legitimacy of governance in any of them before. In each case, the enemies of the U.S.-created governments and their militaries were able to marshal, train, equip, and find sanctuary across a border with a territorial neighbor — Cambodia and North Vietnam in the case of South Vietnam, Syria in the case of Iraq, and Pakistan in the case of Afghanistan.

Thus at the strategic level, the military outcome in Afghanistan is not seriously in question, as there is no strategic basis for it to be different than the outcomes in South Vietnam and Iraq, no matter how much whistling past the strategic graveyard proceeds it. The Afghan National Army (ANA) and Afghan National Police (ANP) cannot maintain security in the southern part of the country after the departure of American forces: Indeed, they are not entirely doing so today. Even while American air power is still available and being applied robustly, at least five Afghan districts have no government presence, and many ANA garrisons in the south and east are already surrounded like little Alamos. Many of these base-bound garrisons are struggling simply to obtain food and ammunition, and they rarely venture outside their perimeters. An hour's drive from Kabul, in Tagab district of Kapisa Province, for example, the soldiers of the ANA garrison are permitted by the Taliban to leave their base for 1 hour each day, to go to the bazaar to buy their food, as long as they carry no weapons.[15] On December 2, 2014, with the help of an ANA defector from the post, the Taliban attacked the ANA outpost Bala Murghab district of Badghis Province[16] almost within sight of the Turkmenistan border and killed the entire garrison of six soldiers.[17] On November 29, 2014, the Taliban overran the ANA garrison in Sangin, Helmand Province, killing 14 ANA soldiers. Another six or seven soldiers were missing in action.[18] The real government in these districts and many, many others today is the Taliban. Momentum is not on the side of the Afghan government, and there is no perceivable "game changer" on the horizon. Slow decay is inevitable, and state failure is a matter of time. Using the metrics in the Central Intelligence Agency's (CIA) unclassified "Guide to the Analysis of Insurgency"[19] and publicly available statistics, it is clear that Afghanistan is in the "final stages of a successful insurgency," (see Appendix I).

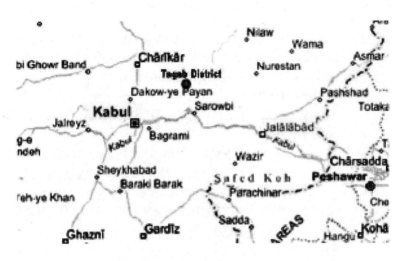

**Map I-1. Afghanistan.**

To assess first the inevitability of state security failure in southern Afghanistan in strictly military terms, a brief summary of the comparative strengths of the security forces of South Vietnam, Iraq, and Afghanistan will provide a useful point of departure.

## RELATIVE GEOGRAPHICAL AND FORCE SIZES

**South Vietnam: 67,108 square miles**
Population (1975): **19.6 million**[20]
Paramilitary:[21] Police, 102,000
Police Field Force, 20,200
Total Paramilitary Police: **122,200**
Other Paramilitary Forces not reporting to the Army of the Republic of Vietnam (ARVN):
People's Self-Defense Force (PSDF), 1,000,000[22] (after 1968)
Revolutionary Development Cadre (RDC), 54,500 (Including Son Thong RDC)
Provincial Reconnaissance Units, 6,000
Kit Carson Scouts, 2,916

Armed Propaganda Teams, 5,550
Total Paramilitary Forces: **1,068,966 = 15.9
militia forces per square mile**
Military:[23]
Army: 710,000 regulars = **10.58 soldiers per
square mile**
> Army: 510,000 Irregulars (Regional Forc-
> es and Provincial Forces, organized into
> 1,500 companies and 8,186 platoons[24])
Navy: 57,000 (Including the 15,000 man
Vietnamese Marine Corps)
Air Force: 63,000
Total Military Forces: **1,340,000 = 20 soldiers
per square mile**

**Security Force Total: 2,531,116 men, 37.71 per sq.
mile, 129.14 per 1,000 citizens**
Percentage of Security Forces comprised by Paramilitary Police: 12.5.

Note: All Civilian Irregular Defense Groups (CIDG)
were transferred into the Border Ranger Battalions of
the ARVN in 1970.

**Afghanistan: 251,827 square miles** (Region-
al Command [RC] South and RC Southwest:
77,869 square miles[25])
> Population (2014): **28.3 million**[26]
Paramilitary: Regular Police, 157,000
Irregular Police, 24,000 (Afghan local police or
ALP)[27]
Public Protection Force (Afghan Public Protec-
tion Force or APPF)[28] 20,000
Total Paramilitary Forces: **201,000 = 0.8 per
square mile**

Military: Army 156,000 regulars in 6 Corps = **0.62 soldiers per square mile**[29]
(The ANA has no reserve or irregular forces associated with it.)

**Security Force Total: 358,000 men, 1.4 per sq. mile 12.8 per 1,000 citizens**
Percentage of Security Forces comprised by Paramilitary Police: 56.

Note: The National Directorate of Security (NDS), the successor to the Soviet *Khadamat-e Aetela'at-e Dawlati* (KHAD) secret police, maintains armed security personnel in each province, possibly totaling 5,000 to 7,000 fighters. The Army number includes the 6,000 men (and approximately 20 women) of the Afghan National Air Force.

**Iraq: 169,234 square miles**
Population (2014): **34.8 million**[30]
Police +/- 25,000: 1 policeman for every 6.8 square miles
Army active duty: 283,000 men in 197 combat battalions
Army reserves: 528,500 men

**Security Force Total: 836,500 men, 4.9 per sq. mile 24.0 per 1,000 citizens**
Percentage of Security Forces comprised by Paramilitary Police: 3.

Note: The 2014 Islamic State of Iraq and Syria (ISIS) offensive struck with such rapidity that effectively none of the reserve forces were mobilized before the collapse of the Iraqi Army. Thus, it could be more accurate to assess that there were 308,000 **armed security providers, or 1.82 per square mile.**

From this statistical comparison, it can be readily seen that of the three countries, in strictly numerical terms, Afghanistan has by far the lowest ratios of armed government security providers per square mile of territory (1.4) and per 1,000 citizens (12.8), and, by an extreme margin, the highest percentage of the state security apparatus comprised of relatively combat-weak police forces (56 percent). The earlier edition of *Field Manual (FM) 3-24/Marine Corps Warfighting Publications (MCWP) 3-33.5, Counterinsurgency,* gave a force density recommendation of 25 security forces per 1,000 citizens, and stated that "20 counterinsurgents per 1,000 residents is often considered the *minimum* troop density required for effective counterinsurgency (COIN) operations."[31]

These numbers were contentious and dropped from the new edition of the manual, and one wonders if the rationale for deleting this formula was a result of South Vietnam having 129 security forces per 1,000 citizens, Iraq having 24 per 1,000 citizens, while Afghanistan has an embarrassingly low 12.8 security personnel per 1,000 citizens, more than half of whom are static and combat-weak police. Force size in counterinsurgency is a hotly debated topic, but until recently, statistical analysis was not available to back up any of the various theories and "rules of thumb." In 2011, however, after an exhaustive empirical study of more than 50 insurgencies using a variety of potential metrics (e.g., number of security forces per square mile, number of security forces per 1,000 population, number of security forces per insurgent, etc.) Jeffrey Friedman of Harvard's Kennedy School concluded that:

force size as measured by troops per inhabitant in the area of operations demonstrates a consistent, positive correlation with counterinsurgents' success in both univariate and multivariate regressions. Troop density also has an advantage over the alternative measures in terms of model fit. This suggests that troops-per-inhabitant is the best way to measure force size in most cases.[32]

Comparing only army forces, the ARVN had **eight and a half times** the number of regular and irregular soldiers that Afghanistan has today (1,340,000 to 157,000), **in a country one-fourth the size**. Their paramilitary police forces were approximately equal in total numbers, but because of South Vietnam's smaller area, the South Vietnamese Police had a force density four times higher than the ANP today. South Vietnam had 1,068,966 men and women in armed militia units, not counting 510,000 regional forces-provincial forces (RF-PFs), who were irregulars formally part of the ARVN. Afghanistan has, on paper, 30,000 — a numerical militia advantage for South Vietnam of 35-to-1, in a country one-fourth the size. For Afghanistan to have the counterinsurgent militia strength today that South Vietnam had per square mile in 1970, there would have to be 4,011,362 men in the ALP. There might be 24,000 ALP actually present.[33] The Iraqi Army, on paper, was twice the size of the ANA, excluding its reserves, with only about 60 percent as much territory to defend. The Iraqi Police were militarily a nonentity. The following sections will now examine qualitative factors.

## COMPARISON OF THE GROUND FORCES

Despite its glaring senior level leadership faults, the ARVN was, in fact, a potent force. As James Willibanks notes:

> South Vietnamese combat strength included about 120 infantry battalion in 11 divisions supported by 58 artillery battalions, 19 battalion-sized armored units, and many engineer and signal formations. By 1972, the regular ARVN divisions were robust organizations with modern equipment and weapons. They included three infantry regiments of three battalions each, one artillery regiment of three battalions, a cavalry squadron, an engineer battalion and various logistics units. In addition to the ARVN divisions, there were 37 border ranger battalions, 21 ranger battalions and the airborne and marine divisions. Complementing the regular forces were the Territorial Forces that included 300,000 Regional Forces and 250,000 Popular Forces (RF/PF) soldiers, and more than 500,000 People's Self-Defense Forces.[34]

The ARVN was thus qualitatively and quantitatively vastly superior to the ANA today. Not counting irregular forces, the ARVN not only numbered over 710,000 regular soldiers, more than four times as many as the ANA, but it also had a country only the size of Regional Command (RC) South and RC Southwest in Afghanistan to defend. A majority of ARVN non-commissioned officers (NCOs) and field-grade commissioned officers fought for the French against the Viet Minh, and many had a decade or more of experience as seasoned soldiers. This is much less true of the ANA. In fact, a deliberate decision was made in the Donald Rumsfeld Department of Defense (DoD) to exclude from the ANA anyone who had ever served in a military-type capacity before, such as former mujahideen, former communist Afghan Army soldiers, and members of warlord militias.[35] The questionnaire for ANA recruits in 2002 (conducted orally, since virtually all recruits were and are illiterate) included the question "Have you ever used a rifle before?" and potential recruits were disqualified if they answered in the affirmative.[36] The future Afghan Army was to be idealistically comprised only of youth who were untainted and uncorrupted by violence. In contrast, from the outset, the ARVN fielded a large number of battle-hardened troops. The ARVN had many excellent combat formations with hundreds of thousands of tough, battle-tested soldiers. In 1975 there were 54 ARVN Ranger Battalions (in Vietnamese, the *Biêt Ðông Quân*) comprising approximately 29,365 men[37] who were as good or better than the equivalent ANA Commandos today.[38] As of June 2014, the ANA has nine commando battalions totaling approximately 10,000 men.[39]

South Vietnamese Rangers were as tough as anything the Viet Cong or the NVA could put in the field. There were 54 battalions of them.

**Picture I-1. South Vietnamese Rangers.**

The ARVN also had a well-developed and functional logistics system, while it is well-documented and widely accepted that the ANA has virtually no logistics capability.[40] As the military proverb runs, "Amateurs talk tactics and professionals talk logistics."[41] The ARVN had an abundance of tactical vehicles, armored personnel carriers, and two-and-a-half-ton trucks; the ANA is hamstrung by vehicle and fuel shortages. As Antonio Giustozzi notes, as much as two-thirds of the fuel delivered to the ANA is being siphoned off by corruption, according to current estimates.[42] The Afghans' ability to keep running the relatively high-maintenance and high-tech vehicles they have inherited from the United States is also limited.[43] In 2014, for example, the Afghan 205 Corps reported that 50 percent of its vehicles were already inoperable.[44] On December 11, 2014, departing International Security Assistance Force (ISAF) Commander Lieutenant General Joseph Anderson told the *Reuters* news agency that Afghan security forces could not perform even basic maintenance. "The problem is you don't have units fixing stuff at their level. This is inept. This is nothing to do with corruption. This is purely ineptitude."[45]

The ARVN also had a full complement of communications gear, down to the platoon level, with well-trained and experienced operators and working tactical codes; the ANA has few radios and communicates largely in the clear with cell phones.[46] In a country where, in many areas, inland waterways were the primary means of transportation, the Vietnamese Navy had absolute brown water supremacy. The ANA, of course, has no navy for obvious reasons, but its ability to keep open even major arteries of the comparable road network of Afghanistan analogous to the rivers and waterways of Vietnam is tenuous at best. The vital Route California in Konar Province, for example, was severed by the Taliban for periods of up to a week on several occasions in 2014.[47]

The ARVN possessed a competent and high-functioning medical corps which provided good quality care to wounded soldiers. In Afghanistan, the 2011 ANA Dawood hospital scandal, when it was discovered that scores of emaciated ANA wounded had died of their wounds for want of food and basic medicines — which the ANA senior medical officer responsible was selling on the black market — speaks for the state of the ANA's marginal medical capability.[48] Compounding the problem, in one of the most disgraceful episodes of the Afghan war, U.S. military officers attempted to cover up the scandal.[49]

The other major components of the ARVN were the RF-PF. The South Vietnamese Popular Force (in Vietnamese, *nghĩa quân*) (sometimes abbreviated SVPF or just PF) consisted of local militias that protected their home villages from attacks by Viet Cong forces and later by People's Army of Vietnam units (PAVN). These forces originally were called the Civil Guard and Self-Defense Corps. The RF (Vietnamese, *địa phuông quân*) were also militias formed in the early-1960s. RF manned a country-wide system of outposts and defended tactically vital points such as bridges and crossroads. The *địa phuông quân* defended approximately 9,000 key terrain features, nearly half of them in the strategically vital Mekong Delta region. In 1964, the RF were integrated into the ARVN and placed under the command of the Joint General Staff. This was vastly more militarily effective than having such militia forces under the control of the Ministry of the Interior (MOI), as is the case in Afghanistan today.

In 1969, with the withdrawal of U.S. forces, the RF became increasingly important, and units began to be attached to ARVN battalions directly, and to deploy with the ARVN outside their home provinces, a significant force multiplier. By 1973, there were 1,810 RF companies of approximately 140 men each.[50] They fought stubbornly, but took heavy casualties. Thomas Thayer, a former analyst in the Secretary of Defense's Office of Systems Analysis, estimates the RF-PFs suffered about 60 percent of the combat casualties within the South Vietnamese security forces and inflicted about 30 percent of enemy casualties.[51] This is indicative of the fact that, like the ALP in Afghanistan, they were intended for local defense, and like the ALP, they were no match for the Viet Cong Main Force and the PAVN, which are the equivalent of the Taliban today. This mismatch in Afghanistan was starkly in evidence again on December 21, 2014, for example, when Taliban guerillas hit an ALP checkpoint in Qashtepa district of Jowzjan province, killing at least seven ALP militia and wounding at least five more.[52]

On an individual soldier level, the overall quality of ANA recruits always has been low and almost all are from the rural areas.[53] This is important because, as the Taliban gains control over more of the rural areas, the number of potential recruits coming from those areas will be curtailed. As Giustozzi noted in 2013, the drive to increase ANA numbers rapidly resulted in the weak vetting of recruits:

> There has been little effort to vet recruits even in terms of physical fitness. Physically weak, drug-addicted and under-motivated recruits have often proved unable to withstand even the rather mild 10-week basic training course.[54]

This in part also fueled a spike in green-on-blue attacks, which drove a wedge of mistrust between ANA soldiers and their mentors. Interviews with ANA recruits have consistently shown the primary motivation to join has always been money.[55] In short, the ARVN was a large, capable, well-equipped, and modern army that could shoot, move, communicate, and sustain. The ANA, one-eighth the size, can barely shoot.

As for Iraq, after Rumsfeld, Douglas Feith, and Paul Bremer made the decision to disband the entire Iraqi Army in May 2003 following the occupation of Baghdad,[56] sending home hundreds of thousands of trained and capable soldiers, NCOs and officers with their weapons, there was never any real possibility of creating a cohesive professional Iraqi Army in the political time frame available. As war correspondent David Axe notes, "Fundamentally, the fault was America's for destroying the existing army, but there was nothing America could do after that to build a truly inclusive and effective new army."[57] The Iraqi Army that was created, armed, and trained for almost a decade by the United States at a cost of some $25 billion dollars[58] disintegrated as a military force within hours in the summer of 2014 at Mosul in the face of a few hundred ISIS irregulars.[59]

## COMPARISON OF THE AIR FORCES

The ARVN also had a powerful air force, the Vietnamese Air Force (VNAF), comprising 2,075 aircraft, including six squadrons of F-8s, and a large force of helicopters, including an impressive Medevac component.[60] It was, at one time, the world's fourth largest air force. Already by 1970, the VNAF was flying over 300,000 sorties per year.[61] In comparison, because then-Secretary of Defense Rumsfeld decreed in 2002 that Afghanistan would have no air force,[62] the existing Afghan National Air Force (ANAF, the term used by the Afghans themselves) languished with only a few decrepit Soviet legacy Mi-24 Hind and Mi-17 Hipp helicopters until 2009, when the Obama administration took office.[63] In 2014, the ANAF flew a total of 7,000 sorties.[64] ISAF flew 133,000, of which 34,000 were for close air support (CAS).[65] In November 2014 the ANAF still had only three Soviet legacy Hind helicopters dedicated to the support of all of RC South, including one (as of October 2014 reporting) down for repairs.

As it stands, very few of the ANAF's current aircraft have operational weapon systems. The ANAF has no operational jets, and currently has no fixed-wing aircraft capable of CAS. It also has no technical or human capability for forward air control.[66] A total of 20 of the sturdy Brazilian-made Embraer A-29 Super Tucano light aircraft (essentially an operationally mature light trainer design in search of a new market) are planned for delivery to the ANAF from 2015 to 2018.[67] The U.S. Air Force (USAF) took delivery of the first aircraft in late-September 2014.[68] This little turbo-prop spotter plane can be armed with two machine guns and two rockets or bombs, and it represents the only significant U.S. commitment to the creation of an organic CAS capability within the ANAF. The ANAF also operates a vague number of MD530f (high altitude) Cayuse Warrior light observation helicopters, perhaps 10 in all, and in the fall of 2014 a $44 million contract was awarded to MD Helicopters to install one .50 caliber (North Atlantic Treaty Organization [NATO] 12.7 x 99 millimeter [mm]) machine gun pod with an ordnance capacity of 400 rounds on each MD530f.[69] An additional 63 well-used and

least one credible but officially unverified report by an American military officer that Pakistani military forces flew multiple helicopter missions to resupply Taliban fighters inside Afghanistan's Nangarhar province in 2007.[78] (From 1996-2001, the Pakistani Air Force maintained and flew aircraft for the Taliban.[79]) The fact that there were jet-to-jet dogfights between the VNAF and the North Vietnamese Air Force (NVAF) should not obscure the fact, however, that the vast preponderance of South Vietnamese air power went to CAS, logistics, resupply, and medevac operations in support of the ARVN, which were **never** interdicted by North Vietnamese aircraft. The VNAF was far superior qualitatively and quantitatively to the NVAF, which until the very end of the war in 1975 did not fly in South Vietnamese air space.[80] The main point to be observed here is that the ARVN had a large, powerful, modern and self-sustaining air force, with 63,000 personnel, 2,075 aircraft, and 72 operational squadrons with total freedom of operation to support ground forces in South Vietnam with more than 300,000 sorties per year. The ANA effectively has none at all.

The Iraqi Air Force is also a military nonentity, with approximately 212 aircraft, virtually none of which are modern or even armed,[81] and 14,000 personnel.[82] When the ISIS terrorist offensive began in June 2014, for all intents and purposes, there was no Iraqi Air Force.[83] This contributed significantly to the collapse of the Iraqi Army itself that summer.[84] The Iraqi Air Force has recently sourced 12 Su-25 Frogfoot attack aircraft from Russia and ordered 36 Lockheed Martin F-16 Block 52 jets but none of these is currently operational.[85] The inclusion of this information on the Iraqi Air Force in this paragraph seems like an afterthought, but the Iraqi Air Force itself was an afterthought.

## COMPARISON OF THE PARAMILITARY POLICE FORCES

For good reasons, police forces are not generally considered to be a part of the equation in calculating military outcomes, and those of South Vietnam and Iraq were no exception. Police are, by definition, a law enforcement mechanism, and one not structured, trained, or equipped to perform as light infantry. Their combat power is so negligible that no one has ever invented a military tactical symbol for a police company (see Appendix II). Third World police forces like the ANP are illiterate and innumerate, corrupt, lightly armed, and barely trained to maintain civil order. Their primary "security" function is to man roadblocks, search vehicles for weapons and explosives, and act as a "tripwire" for enemy attacks, relying on reinforcements from nearby army garrisons for support in *extremis*. As will be seen, the ANP fail at even these basic tasks, and there is little cooperation with the ANA.

Tough Police Field Force (PFF) troopers before a joint operation with the ARVN. Note the camouflage fatigues, camouflaged helmets, and tracking dogs. The PFF used the dogs to aggressively track insurgents and engage them. The ANSF don't touch dogs, believing them unclean, and rarely, if ever pursue insurgents.

**Picture I-3. PFF Troops before a Joint Operation with the ARVN.**

The police in South Vietnam, on the other hand, included a number of capable paramilitary police forces, including combat police with armored fighting vehicles. Together, they comprised 12.5 percent of the overall security forces. In Afghanistan, the paramilitary police forces, including the lightly armed ANP, comprise 56 percent of the security forces. Historically, the police forces of South Vietnam and Iraq were military nonentities in the collapse of those countries in 1975 and 2014, respectively, and the same will be true of Afghanistan.

The police forces of the Republic of [South] Vietnam included the National Police or RVNP (in Vietnamese the *Cãnh lúc Quôc gia Viêt Nam Công hòa*), the Rural Development Cadres, Provincial Reconnaissance Units, Kit Carson Scouts (Viet Cong defectors), and most significantly an elite, division-sized quick-reaction police unit known as the Republic of Vietnam National Police Field Force (in Vietnamese, the *Cãnh Sát Dã Chiên* or CSDC). None of these valuable counterinsurgency units have any equivalent in the ANP today. The CSDC was largely comprised of tough, experienced professionals, many of whom had been fighting communist guerillas since the days of the French colonial regime in the 1950s. By August 1971, CSDC strength was 16,500 officers and enlisted men organized into 44 provincial battalions with 90 companies, 242 district platoons and an independent armored cavalry platoon.[86]

Overall, there were 17.75 counterinsurgent paramilitary forces (paramilitary police, PSDF, RF-PF, and other paramilitary forces) per square mile in South Vietnam, compared to 0.8 paramilitary forces (paramilitary police and ANP) per square mile in Afghanistan today. In other words, in every 10 square mile area of South Vietnam, there were 177 paramilitary forces; in Afghanistan there are eight, an RVNP numerical advantage of over 22:1. Importantly, the entire operational area of the RVNP was 10,000 square miles **smaller** than just RC South and RC Southwest combined in Afghanistan today, permitting much faster response times by security forces. Furthermore, man for man, the South Vietnamese police were a better paramilitary force than the ANP, with higher literacy (adult literacy in South Vietnam in the 1970s was approximately 80 percent[87]), far more average years of experience per patrolman, better equipment, lower attrition, better training, and better pay. Overall adult literacy is about 25 percent in Afghanistan today.[88] This means most police and paramilitary forces in South Vietnam were literate, while few in Afghanistan are, as a result of intense private sector competition there for literate employees.

CẢNH SÁT QUỐC GIA
THI HÀNH CÔNG TÁC
KIỂM SOÁT TÀI NGUYÊN
ĐỂ PHỤC VỤ ĐỒNG BÀO

Cảnh Sát Quốc Gia thi hành công tác kiểm soát tài nguyên mục đích giữ gìn những tài nguyên Quốc Gia không để lọt

Because of high literacy levels in Vietnam, such leaflets could have an effect.

**Picture I-4. South Vietnamese Propaganda Leaflet.**

Attrition is a serious problem for the ANP. ANP desertion rates are difficult to come by and even more difficult to verify. The Congressional Research Service reported on December 2, 2014, that ANP desertions are "far higher than that of the ANA."[89] Giustozzi and Mohammed Isaqzadeh note that attrition in the spring of 2010 was running at 70 percent, dropping to an annualized 60 percent by November.[90] In Helmand Province in 2008-09, annual ANP attrition was 57 percent, of which 45 percent was a result of desertions and 12 percent a result of combat casualties.[91] The U.S. Institute for Peace (USIP), however, cites a figure of 25 percent.[92] A reasonable hybrid estimate of police attrition through desertions, weighted for methodology and reliability, would be about 50 percent per year.

Because annual attrition runs at 50 percent, most ANP patrolmen have little training and little tactical skill. There were so many accidents in training that ANP trainees are given wooden guns, above. Because of reliability issues, when they graduate to real guns, they are not given bullets (Barcroft Media/Daily Mail).

**Picture I-5. Training of ANP Patrolmen.**

Police forces in all three countries were and are plagued by uneven and politicized leadership, and by a debilitating reputation for corruption. A report released by SIGAR on January 12, 2015, found that there were 152,678 ANP formally on the rolls[93] but twice that many ANP identification cards are in circulation. To put it bluntly, no one has any idea how many ANP there actually are, and SIGAR noted that the 152,678 number is largely guesswork. In its in-person 2011 audit of ANP personnel, SIGAR found personnel numbers "ranging from 111,774 to 125,218, a discrepancy of 13,444 personnel."[94] Personnel accountability of the ANP has been a chronic problem since its inception.[95]

Some percentage of the ANP number consists of nonexistent personnel, or "ghost policemen." How large is the "ghost policeman" problem? No one knows. In 2006, 20 percent of reported ANP personnel were found to be nonexistent by the Inspectors General for the Departments of State and Defense in a joint report.[96] In 2009, the number had risen to 30 percent, or 25,000 phantom policemen, according to a U.S. embassy cable cited by the U.S. Government Accountability Office.[97] The embassy cable reported that police chiefs all over Afghanistan were "creating 'ghost policemen'" in order to collect their salaries. As SIGAR noted:

> Most recently, in August 2014, the Department of Defense Office of Inspector General reported that the MOI processed 4,579 potentially improper salary payments totaling $40 million due to the ministry's lack of procedures to identify improper payments, such as duplicate payments. The Department of Defense Inspector General also found that MOI officials did not follow payroll procedures and modified payroll documents after the documents had been approved and signed.[98]

If the 30 percent "ghost policeman" rate has not improved since 2009, and in January 2014 SIGAR reported no reason to believe it has, then the ANP in January 2015 has a total of approximately 107,000 actual personnel. In June 2014, about half of the ANP consisted of actual enlisted "patrolmen" in the field.[99] Thus a reasonable estimate of the number of ANP actually in the field in Afghanistan today with guns in their hands would be 53,500 men. About 27,000 of them desert and have to be replaced each year; another 4,000 are killed in action. As a result, the average level of training per patrolman, years of experience per patrolman, and literacy per patrolman is very low.

Security is not simply a numbers game. It is dangerous, even intellectually dishonest, to count such poorly armed and poorly trained paramilitary personnel as "security forces" in any but the lowest threat security environments, such as, for example, Indian Kashmir today. In 2013, the Taliban launched 6,604 operations, 50 suicide attacks, and 1,704 direct attacks on police,[100] killing at least 4,000 policemen.[101] Approximately 2,000 police checkpoints in Afghanistan were overrun by Taliban hit-and-run attacks in 2014. Most of them were subsequently reestablished nearby, but this entirely misses the point. The Taliban's tactics are not intended to take and hold rural checkpoints, they are intended to inflict steady casualties on the police and intimidate and demoralize the force. In the insurgency in Jammu and Kashmir, in comparison, there were 17 attacks on security forces in 2014, causing 11 deaths.[102] This is the level of insurgency at which vertically integrated policing and other paramilitary forces are effective, not 1,700 attacks.

In a full-blown insurgency like Vietnam and Afghanistan, police add so little to the overall military balance that their inclusion gives little more than a false sense of security from force numbers, which appear larger without adding any real combat capability. The Taliban are not bicycle thieves or farmers fighting over water rights, they are heavily armed and highly motivated guerillas akin to the Viet Cong Main Force and the PAVN. Indeed, in the final stages of a successful insurgency, as defined by the CIA and as Afghanistan is in now,[103] the police are essentially stationary targets providing a source of free weapons, ammunition and equipment for the guerrillas. Using the CIA's "Guide to the Analysis of Insurgency," from the high ANP casualty and desertion rates and the number of direct attacks on the police this year, it is clear that in 2014 the ANP are already in over their heads militarily in the "late stage of a successful insurgency,"[104] (see Appendix I).

Taliban fighters, top (Reuters/Wahdat). Mixed group of Viet Cong and PAVN troops, bottom.

**Picture I-6. Taliban Fighters and a Mixed Group of Viet Cong and PAVN Troops.**

The ability of the ANP to carry out sustained resistance in the face of a determined and numerically superior enemy force in rural areas is very limited. The ANP are, in fact, a net security negative, in the sense that their existence contributes more overall to insecurity than to security.

There are four basic components of this overall net negative rating: First, their corruption alienates the local population and spurs Taliban recruiting.[105] A recent survey found the level of confidence in the ANP in the Pashtun provinces of Kandahar, Zabul, and Paktika was below 25 percent,[106] and half of all Afghans interviewed said they had personally experienced police corruption.[107] Police corruption has been frequently cited as one of the most common causes of popular support and recruiting for the Taliban.[108] Their corruption may well be creating more Taliban than they are taking off the field in combat. That alone would make them a net security negative. As the Marine Lieutenant Colonel heading the police advisory group in Sangin in 2013 noted, "If you shut down all their corruption schemes, the police would cease to exist." He noted with obvious frustration that the local police chief is "a murderer and child molester" who "treats the people of Sangin as his personal piggy-bank." The Marine reported all of this up the chain of command, and, reporter Ben Anderson observed, "Nothing was ever done." "Having to work with people like this," the Marine officer said, "[in order] to get the mission done . . . kind of wears on you."[109]

Second, their ubiquitous, system-wide focus on taking bribes means little actual added security. Police "checkpoints" (usually a rock or two in the middle of the road) are almost universally the venue for shaking down motorists and truck drivers for bribes. The security function of these checkpoints is routinely negated when 10 rupees will bypass the requirement for an inspection of passengers and cargo. Anyone moving insurgent leaders or materiel by car or truck simply pays the bribe.

Above, an Afghan National Policeman taking a routine bribe from a truck driver not to inspect the cargo, caught on a CBS News surveillance video. Below, an ANP patrolman takes a bribe from a pedestrian not to search him. This universal behavior simply alienates the people and is "security" (as in "ANSF") in name only.

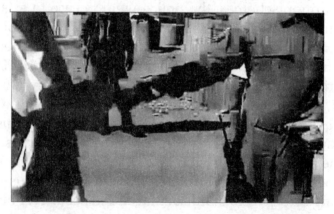

**Picture I-7. ANP Patrolmen Taking Bribes
Not to Inspect Cargo or Pedestrians.**

Third, their casualties demoralize civilians inclined to support the government. The ANP are being liquidated systematically, and the local civilian population sees this. An average of 11 ANP personnel are killed **every day** as stationary targets in indefensible fixed positions.[110] For example, four policemen were captured and later murdered in Wardak province on January 3, 2015, by a Taliban battle group.[111] On January 4, 2015, five more were attacked and killed by a much larger Taliban force in Baraki Barak district of Logar province.[112] On January 12, 2015, the Police Chief of Mazan district in Zabul province was killed, along with two of his bodyguards.[113] In December 2014, ANP casualties were at an all-time high.[114] Almost 3,000 ANP were killed in action in 2013, and 3,500 were killed in action in the first 10 months of 2014, suggesting the 2014 year-end ANP killed in action (KIA) statistic reached 4,000.[115] At least 12,000 more were wounded.[116] Many ANP units in the south and southwest and even northern Kapisa province are engaged in combat with jihadists on an almost daily basis.[117] In fact, the insurgency has grown far beyond anything these untrained and lightly armed constabularies can cope with.

Fourth, their passive, static nature and easily overrun positions are a free arsenal from which the Taliban can acquire more weapons, ammunition, and equipment. In military terms, in a high-threat environment as Afghanistan is now, a static force focused on defending its own positions contributes little to the battlefield. The ANP have little mobility, very little firepower, are dependent on the local community for logistics, and have little or no initiative and offensive spirit. In the *Armed Forces Journal* in 2012, for example, Lieutenant Colonel Daniel L. Davis reported American troops in Kunar province as saying the ANP rarely leave their checkpoints.[118] Following one Taliban attack on a police checkpoint, Davis himself asked the police commander if he regularly pursued attacking insurgents. The ANP commander looked at him "with an incredulous expression" then laughed and replied, "No, we don't go after them. That would be dangerous!"[119] Counting the ANP as "ANSF" is a chimera, and lumping them into a larger "security forces" number as equal and interchangeable units with a value of "one" is willful self-deception (see Appendix II).

In comparison, the Iraqi Police Service (IPS) numbered on paper approximately 25,000 policemen in 2007, of whom about a third were on leave at any given time.[120] The police forces in Iraq only comprised about 3 percent of the overall security forces. At the time of the U.S. invasion, Iraq had one of the highest male literacy rates in the Middle East,[121] and most Iraqi policemen were literate. Iraq had no government-recognized paramilitary forces. In 2014, during the advance of the terrorist organization known as ISIS, the IPS disintegrated within minutes wherever the two forces came into contact, the IPS often fleeing in their vehicles ahead of the ISIS lead elements. In an overall comparison of the capability of the police forces in these three countries to maintain civil order in rural areas and act as paramilitary first-responders to insurgent attacks, the RVNP ranks first by a wide margin, followed far behind by the ANP. In the collapse of the security forces in both Vietnam and Iraq, the Vietnamese police and the IPS were militarily insignificant. This in particular bodes poorly for the situation in Afghanistan, where in comparison to Iraq (3 percent) and Vietnam (12.5 percent), the weak paramilitary police comprise 56 percent of the security providers in the overall force (see Appendix II).

The failure of the police to be able to match up to the threat is another lesson unlearned from the Vietnam war. The challenges facing both police trainers and policymakers in South Vietnam **in the early-1960s** are so strikingly relevant to the situation in Afghanistan today that they bear quoting at length:

> The growth of the insurgency created a dilemma for American police advisors. As eager as they were to develop civilian law enforcement institutions, they also recognized that lightly armed police, particularly in the countryside, the area of the insurgency's greatest strength, were likely to be overwhelmed by aggressive and disciplined communist guerilla forces. American military critics of police-oriented counter-insurgency strategies had argued that police and paramilitary forces were no match for the PLAF [People's Liberation Armed Forces]. American police advisors eventually reached the same conclusion. The Viet Cong's strength was apparent every time PSD [personal security detail] personnel left Saigon. Guerilla ambushes were a routine feature of the environment in Vietnam's hinterlands. Few civilian police were operating in rural areas, but what few there were encountered a communist adversary who was often better trained and equipped. Villages controlled by the PAVN were virtually no-go areas for Diem's law enforcement agencies. The Civil Guard, Self-Defense Corps (SDC) and village militias were receiving generous American assistance to provide security for the Strategic Hamlet Program. The paramilitary forces, however, failed to halt communist violence in the countryside.[122]

The lack of cooperation between the ANP and the ANA is a major area of security failure. The ANA rarely acts in concert with ANP, and the antagonism between them has sharply reduced security levels. In late-December 2014, *The New York Times* quoted an ANP patrolman named Mohammad Saleh as saying

"The army rarely conducts joint operations with the police, leaving [the police] to do most of the fighting." Another policeman added "Only the asphalt road is under the control of the government in Sangin. Everything else is Taliban."[123] In November 2014, *Stars and Stripes* reporter Josh Smith observed in Laghman province what was supposed to be a joint ANA/ANP operation. The ANA were firing a 122-mm Soviet artillery piece more or less at random toward a police operation a mile or two away. Later in the day while the police were still engaging insurgents with small arms, the ANA packed up and went home without telling the police.[124]

In some parts of the country, this lack of cooperation results in armed conflict between the ANA and the ANP. In the summer of 2014, for example, combat between the ANA and the ANP occurred in Helmand province.[125] The failure of the ANA and ANP to cooperate and coordinate security does not bode well for the longevity of the security forces, and it is such a severe problem today that it has recently received attention from both the outgoing ISAF commander and Afghan President Ashraf Ghani. In December 2014, departing Commander of ISAF Lieutenant General Joseph Anderson noted the Ministry of Defense and the Ministry of Interior need to figure out how to cooperate—when new Ministers are approved and sworn into office. "Right now they don't have the forces," Anderson noted, "and they don't have the cooperation between the entities."[126] Afghan news source *TOLO News* reported on December 16, 2014, that:

> in a meeting with Afghan National Army officers in Kabul, [President Ashraf] Ghani . . . stressed there was a lack of coordination between the Ministry of De-

fense, Ministry of Interior, and the National Directorate of Security.[127]

On December 11, Anderson added: "You've got a
mix right now of uniform police, civil obedience police, and the army, all in the same footprint debating
over who's got primacy for responsibility. That's a
fundamental issue here."[128] The outgoing head of the
European Union (EU) Police Mission in Afghanistan
(EUPOL), Karl Ake Roghe, said in December 2014:

> This is the main problem for Afghanistan—how they
> are dividing the responsibilities for fighting the insur-
> gency. This should be a task for the Afghan National
> Army, not the police. Currently it belongs to the police
> and the main part of the fight is done by the police. . . .
> They are doing this totally alone, and, of course, they
> are not properly equipped for this task.[129]

Even when the army is inclined to support the police, the ANA's relative lack of tactical mobility and
firepower has made it difficult for the Afghan Army
to reinforce the ANP quickly. In addition, in Afghanistan, the police are armed with the AK-47 family of
rifles, firing 7.62-mm caliber ammunition; while the
ANA is now equipped with the M-16 family of rifles,
chambering 5.56-mm ammunition. As a result, the
ANA and the ANP cannot share ammunition, so that
when the ANA are called in to support ANP garrisons
or outposts under attack, if the ANA respond at all,
they cannot resupply the police with ammunition, a
tactical interoperability failure with major operational
implications.

However, in some areas, ANP performance is better than ANA performance, and they are more reliable. Two American Special Forces personnel were

killed and another four wounded in the Tagab district center of Kapisa Province 50 miles east of Kabul in February 2014 by a green-on-blue attack. The area is riddled with Taliban as *The New York Times* reports:[130]

> American Special Forces soldiers who have operated in the area describe a disciplined Taliban force that has been able to operate freely. Its ability to issue and execute orders is exacting, and ambushes are orchestrated with precision.[131]

The performance of the ANA in the district was described as "lackluster," and it was determined that the ANA was so thoroughly infiltrated by the Taliban that the decision was made to cease operations with them and try working with the ANP garrison there instead.[132] In Tagab and elsewhere, however, the ANP lack the firepower, manpower, and willpower to take the fight to the enemy. *The New York Times* reporter present in a skirmish in November 2014 reported that the ANP fought a static, defensive battle:

> As the firing continued and drew closer, the Afghan forces threw everything they had at the insurgents. They lobbed grenades, fired rockets, and emptied clips, but never left the road . . . for the most part, they refused to enter the valley and pursue the Taliban.[133]

The point to be observed here is simply that, in a comparison of the post-U.S. departure environments of South Vietnam, Iraq, and Afghanistan for purposes of assessing outcomes, the paramilitary forces of South Vietnam were far superior, qualitatively and quantitatively, to those of Afghanistan today, and they comprised only a small fraction of the overall force. In Afghanistan, they are more than half the force. Those of Iraq were irrelevant.

# COMPARISON OF THE IRREGULAR FORCES

South Vietnam had a very large and comparatively well-equipped and well-organized body of irregulars, some of whom had embedded U.S. advisors for years as part of the Marine Corps' Combined Action Platoon (CAP) program instituted by Marine General Walt in I Corps.[134] The ARVN could depend on local support from some 510,000 RF-PFs (or "ruff-puffs" as they were referred to in the argot of the time), and vice versa. The RF-PFs were similar in concept to the ALP now being hastily established as a part of the Village Stability Operations (VSO) underway today in Afghanistan, but critically, in terms of their effectiveness and sustainment, they were a part of the Ministry of Defense. In Afghanistan, these forces are illogically and inefficiently connected to the police and the faraway (and notoriously corrupt) MOI in Kabul, rather than to the local ANA battalion, making close operational cooperation with the ANA difficult or impossible. In Vietnam, the paramilitary wiring diagram was more logically and more efficiently vertically integrated to the ARVN and the Ministry of Defense. In South Vietnam, both the regular army and the irregulars (such as the ALP would be considered) were in the same chain of command and had interoperable weapons and communications equipment. In Afghanistan, the ALP are expressly prohibited from participating in offensive actions.[135]

In both Vietnam and Afghanistan, however, the overall number of village defense groups supported by embedded American forces was and is limited; in Vietnam by the relatively small size of the Marine Corps' CAP program in I Corps, and the unwillingness of the U.S. Army to have any part of the program,[136] and in

Afghanistan by the limited number of Special Forces/ Special Operations Forces (SF/SOF) teams available. Once again, as in 2005, current requirements in Iraq for these "high demand, low density" forces are having an impact on the VSO effort in Afghanistan by reducing the number of SF/SOF personnel available. In many areas of Afghanistan, the VSO teams, or "platforms," have already "thinned up," (i.e., moved up to the district center level of operations from the village level) as part of the operating concept to "shape, hold, build, expand, and transition."[137] The CAP program was highly successful because it was connected directly to the ARVN and the Marine Corps in I Corps.[138] As Max Boot notes, "No village protected under CAP was ever retaken by the Viet Cong."[139] The same cannot be said of the ALP.

Roughly similar levels of effort were expended in Vietnam and Afghanistan to create such secure hamlets and, in theory, gradually expand them together into ink blots of territory in armed opposition to the insurgents. Overall, in strategic terms, the scale of these operations in comparison to the sizes of the countries and the percentages of villages engaged, however, could best be described as "experimental." There are approximately 60,000 villages in Afghanistan in 410 districts,[140] and the VSO program is authorized to conduct operations in approximately 100 districts. The exact number of villages in the program is not publicly available, but a design force size of 30 men per village and 300 men per district is standard.[141] Given an overall program force size of 30,000 men, a total of approximately 1,000 villages could be involved, or proportionally 10 per district in each of the approximately 100 districts authorized.[142] That would correspond to about 1/60th of all the villages in Afghanistan.

ALP forces in Sar Hawza District of Paktika Province, where the author served, in 2011. One elder, seven boys and five rifles. This is what is supposed to stop the Taliban. Photo by Heidi Voight/AP.

**Picture I-8. ALP Forces in Sar Hawza District.**

The CAP program that supported the PSDF and the RF-PFs was limited to the operational area of the Marines in I Corps, the northernmost of four Corps in South Vietnam, with regional responsibility shared with the Army, because the Army had no interest in the program. Instead, American SF/SOF personnel operated with the Civilian Irregular Defense Groups (CIDG), which were converted into ARVN Border Ranger Battalions in 1970 and hence are not considered here. The size of the Combined Action Platoon program reached its maximum size in 1970 at four Groups with 114 companies of approximately 100 men each spread throughout the five provinces of I Corps.[143]

As a military comparison, the RF-PFs were certainly more numerous (510,000 men), more capable, better disciplined, and better organized than the somewhat comparable ALP forces (maximum 30,000 men) being created as quickly as possible in parts of southern Afghanistan. The RF-PFs inflicted about 30 percent of the casualties suffered by the Viet Cong.[144] In Afghanistan, by January 2012, there were 57 validated districts in which approximately 11,066 ALP operated. The MOI subsequently approved the recruitment of 30,000 ALP to serve in 99 of 410 districts throughout the country,[145] and that goal has apparently been reached on paper. However, public estimates of the actual size of the ALP and the VSO program are sharply divergent. *The Long War Journal*, for example, stated on March 28, 2013, that there were:

> currently . . . about 70 VSO sites, and each site consists of approximately 12 local police. The total force in Afghanistan to date is about 800 local police and is a far cry from the proposed 10,000 sought out by President Karzai and NATO/ISAF forces.[146]

It is difficult to see how it would be possible to grow from 360 men (70 sites x 12 men each) in March 2013 or even "800 men"[147] to 30,000 men 18 months later.

It should be noted that the ALP is simply the latest in a long and muddled history of such intermittent, half-hearted, short-lived, and unsuccessful U.S. military experiments with irregular forces unwisely connected to the MOI in Afghanistan,[148] including Community-Based Security Solutions (CBSS), the Critical Infrastructure Protection (CIP) Program, Intermediate Security for Critical Infrastructure (ISCI), the Afghan Public Protection Program (AP3), and Local Security Forces (LSF). The last category includes unlicensed private security companies, militias, and *Arbakai* forces still in operation as of 2012.[149] Not included here are the CIA's notoriously renegade and above-the-law[150] Counterterrorist Pursuit Teams in the Kunar region,[151] the 3,500 man Khost Protection Force (KPF)[152] and the Cultural Exploitation Units (CEUs). One of the most notorious, the Kandahar Strike Force, has been repeatedly accused of human rights violations and described as "the most shadowy and the most unaccountable in the country."[153] The KPF once attacked a police station in Kandahar and killed the ANP police chief in order to break one of their militiamen out of jail who was awaiting trial for murder.[154]

These efforts have been consistently carried out against the advice of many Afghanistan experts, who correctly pointed out that unless these forces were incorporated into the ANA in some fashion, rather than functioning as stand-alone "police" forces loosely connected to the local police and thence to the distant and infamously corrupt MOI, the ALP would soon devolve into warlord militias committing human rights abuses, including extrajudicial killings. That is exactly what has happened.[155] "Not only do they murder," as Dexter Filkins notes, "they also steal, tax, and rape."[156] The Congressional Research Service notes that "the ALP program has been cited by Human Rights Watch and other human rights groups for killings, rapes, arbitrary detentions, and land grabs."[157] Oxfam added child sexual abuse to the list.[158] The allegations were frequent enough that the U.S. Government was forced to launch an investigation into the abuses and found many of them credible.[159] In May 2011, Oxfam reported that design procedures and community protections built into the program on paper are often circumvented on the ground[160] and warned of "communities living in fear of government-supported community defense initiatives they see as criminal gangs."[161] As the United Nations Assistance Mission in Afghanistan (UNAMA) reported:

> UNAMA observed weaknesses in the recruitment, vetting, training and discipline of ALP as local communities in some areas reported ALP involvement in criminality and serious human rights violations, including the displacement of civilians, abduction, physical and sexual abuse, and extortion. UNAMA observed . . . a lack of accountability and oversight of some ALP operations. In addition, despite procedures for the vetting of individuals required to be conducted by local *shuras*, UNAMA observed that in some areas local power brokers influenced which individuals were nominated and ratified as ALP members with some individuals with documented human rights abuses joining the ALP. In some cases, the ALP did not appear to reflect the ethnic balance in the areas they operated adding to tensions within communities. In some areas, former illegal armed groups were absorbed into ALP raising concerns in local communities that the ALP was used to legitimize such individuals and their activities.[162]

On July 4, 2012, *The Washington Post* reported an ALP unit of 41 men in Badghis had defected *en masse* to the Taliban.[163] In June 2013, another ALP unit of six men in Panirak village of Bala Murghab district of Badghis province also joined Taliban militants, taking their weapons and equipment with them.[164] Other ALP militias are making deals with the Taliban they were supposed to fight. In October 2014, for example, it was reported by the *Guardian* newspaper that the ALP unit in the Gizab District of Uruzgan Province — once specifically touted as the showpiece of the ALP and VSO programs in Afghanistan[165] — has done exactly that. The Taliban has reestablished control over 80 percent of the district.[166] In November 2014, ALP units in Logar, Maidan, Wardak, and Ghazni provinces, which have gone unpaid by the Afghan government for months, were reported to be selling their weapons and ammunition to the Taliban to feed their families.[167]

Like the ANP, the ALP has also been forced into conflict beyond its design parameters and tactical abilities and is over its head. As *Stars and Stripes* reporter Josh Smith notes:

> The ALP was initially envisioned as a sort of national guard that would live at home until called out, [but] the high demands of the unending violence [have] forced many ALP to man checkpoints and other bases around the clock.[168]

Having been pushed into this battle by the VSO program, they are now marked for death by the Taliban[169] and they are on their own. Haji Iqbal, an ALP commander in Dowlat Shah district of Laghman province, says they have received no support from the Afghan government. "Communities are paying for this themselves," Haji Iqbal said, "and the lack of resources means they are often outgunned by the enemy."[170] Haji Noorani, an ALP commander in neighboring Alishang district, agrees. "If the current situation continues, the whole province will eventually return to the Taliban," Noorani said, adding, "the politicians say all is well, but it is not true."[171]

Entropy, or gradual decline into disorder, is the second law of thermodynamics but the first law of Afghan security. It is a fact that counterinsurgency is a dirty business, and, as many writers have noted, there are few "good guys" in Afghanistan.[172] It is also true that guerilla warfare cannot be won by bureaucrats in Washington fighting by the Marquis of Queensbury's Rules.[173] But by any reasonable standard, police-based irregulars in Afghanistan like the ALP and their pre-decessors have a dismal track record in the business of winning hearts and minds. They are a poor idea being stubbornly pursued by American military leaders in Special Operations Command (SOCOM) with a thimbleful of Afghan cultural knowledge, a hagiographic view of Special Forces, and a seemingly perverse bent to explore every possible iteration of getting irregular forces wrong.

## STRATEGIC IMPACT OF IRREGULARS

In South Vietnam and in Afghanistan and Iraq today, there are ethnic groups, tribes, and clans that were or are staunchly opposed to the insurgents and that fought or are fighting desperately to prevent an insurgent takeover of their lands, fearing in many cases genocidal retribution if they fail. In Vietnam, these included the Hmong and the Montanyards of the highlands; in Iraq today the Kurds and the Yazidi minority community; and in Afghanistan, they include several disenfranchised Pashtun tribes with long-standing antipathies to the Taliban tribes, the Shi'a Hazara ethnic group, and much of the Dari- and Uzbek-speaking population in the northern areas.

For example, the Mashwari (or Meshwari) tribe of Dangam district of Konar province has been "rabidly anti-Taliban" for many years.[174] According to the Office of the United Nations High Commissioner for Refugees (UNHCR) this animosity precedes the attacks of September 11, 2001, in the United States.[175] In late-November and early-December 2014, it was reported that there was a "tribal uprising" against the Pakistani Taliban (*Tehrik-i-Taliban Pakistan*, or TTP) in Dangam district.[176] The Mashwari receive military support by being members of an ALP militia in Dangam district.

It would be incorrect to attribute the "uprising" to a yearning on the part of the people of Dangam district to be free from the Taliban and to support the national government, however. In actuality, the Mashwari are one of two major tribes in the district. The other tribe, the Salazai, have been at war with the Mashwari for decades, and they receive military support in exchange for loyalty and fealty to the Taliban.[177] Thus each side has forged an outside military alliance, a common practice in the feuds of the Afghan hills. The conflict in Dangam district is thus a tribal war, not a government vs. insurgents war. The Mashwari do not want to kill Taliban, they want to kill Salazai.

Historically, such irregular forces were a militarily insignificant part of South Vietnamese resistance to invasion from the north. For the first 6 months of the ISIS terrorist offensive in Iraq, the Kurdish militias (collectively termed the *Peshmerga*) struggled to protect their own ethnic communities, and only in mid-December 2014 began to push back into ISIS-held territory — with the help of heavy U.S. air support.[178]

Most importantly, between 1996 and 2001 in Afghanistan, irregulars akin to the ALP today loosely allied under the banner of the Northern Alliance, without tactical exception, proved to be unable to defeat the Taliban and hold their ground. From 1996 to 2001, Northern Alliance irregulars often fought stubbornly, but were always on the defensive, fighting holding actions and retrograde movements. Once outside the territory of their own clans, they often ceased fighting, a universal characteristic of conflict in Afghanistan.[179] They were ultimately betrayed by Uzbek commander Abdul Malik Pahlawan and his Uzbek militiamen from the Uzbek *Junbish* party (*Junbish-e Milli-i Islami-i Afghanistan*). Ismael Khan was captured, and Abdul Rashid Dostum escaped to Turkey. By July 2001, the

Northern Alliance had yielded control of virtually all of Afghanistan to the Taliban. Afghan history shows that tribal irregulars cannot hold back, let alone reverse, the momentum of religious movements like the Taliban.

In Iraq today, only larger and more ethnically cohesive irregulars such as the Kurdish *Peshmerga*, which received virtually no support and training from the United States prior to 2014, constitute meaningful resistance to ISIS. The extent to which U.S. Army training and equipment increases a fragile foreign government's chances of survival is debatable: the U.S.-trained and equipped Iraqi Army collapsed in a matter of hours during the ISIS offensive in the summer of 2014, while the Kurds, a downtrodden and persecuted minority in three countries that received no U.S. military support prior to 2014, are putting up a stiff resistance in Iraq and Syria today. The difference is that the Kurds think of themselves as a nation and are willing to fight and die for it. There is no substitute for nationhood, a concept that will be explored in depth in Part II.

## MILITARY CONCLUSIONS REGARDING COMPARABLE FORCE SIZES

The point here is not to belabor the comparison of the equivalent Afghan, Iraqi, and South Vietnamese army, paramilitary, and local irregular forces. Rather, the four key points to consider are these:

1. All of the security forces of all types of South Vietnam and the Iraqi Army were qualitatively and quantitatively vastly superior to those in Afghanistan today, and both quickly collapsed for reasons that will be discussed in Part II.

2. All of the militia-type forces in South Vietnam and Iraq (the *Peshmerga*) were far larger in size, better equipped, better mentored, and better trained than the paramilitary ANP is today, but they did not play any militarily significant role in the events of 1975 and 2014. The ANP, which comprises more than half the ANSF on paper (56 percent), is already overmatched by numerically superior and better-armed Taliban combat groups, is taking heavy casualties as a result, and is a net security negative (see Appendix II). Similarly, the ANP will play no militarily significant role in the events of 2015-19. Counting them as "security forces" is intellectually dishonest.

3. All of the security forces in South Vietnam, Iraq, and the Northern Alliance from 1996 to 2001 were far superior qualitatively and quantitatively in numbers and equipment to those of the ANSF today, and all three were roundly defeated on the battlefield.

4. The security forces of South Vietnam in 1975 outnumbered those in Afghanistan **today** 28-to-1 per square mile, and 5.4-to-1 per 1,000 inhabitants. South Vietnam lost.

In conclusion, the military, paramilitary police forces, and irregulars in South Vietnam and Iraq in 1975 and 2014, respectively, and in Afghanistan from 1996-2001, were simply no match for the disciplined, mobile, highly motivated, battle-tested, and more heavily armed troops they faced and still face today, whether they were ISIS, the Viet Cong main force, the PAVN, the Taliban, or the North Vietnamese Army (NVA). In terms of objective analysis, there is no realistic military possibility that the undersized and underequipped "ANSF," lacking CAS, logistics, and medical support, and disproportionately comprised of combat-weak police, will fare better than the ARVN, the Iraqi Army, the Soviet-Afghan army, or the Northern Alliance.

## CLOSE AIR SUPPORT: THE *SINE QUA NON* OF AFGHAN NATIONAL SECURITY FORCES SURVIVAL

As has been discussed, the ANAF does not currently have any aircraft equipped to conduct CAS, the ANA does not have a single Forward Air Controller (FAC) trained to call for it, and the only capability currently in the pipeline for the ANAF is 20 light A-29 Super Tucano trainers adapted to carry an ordnance load-out of two wing-mounted machine guns and two bombs or rockets.[180]

CAS is one of the most difficult functions of a modern military force. Even with extensive and recurring training and practice, there are often tragic mistakes, such as the one that killed five American soldiers in Zabul province in June 2014.[181] The basic building blocks of competent close air support are aircraft designed for the mission, like the A-10 Warthog, highly numerate and well-educated FAC officers with months of training in specialized schools, advanced communications equipment with encrypted transmissions to prevent enemy countermeasures, and sophisticated methods of target designation and marking. The ability to operate advanced global positioning system equipment and maps, make accurate calculations of enemy positions, calculate aircraft approach vectors, determine the location and proximity of all friendly troops on a constantly shifting battlefield, and communicate calmly and clearly while under enemy fire does not come easily, and it is beyond anything the Afghans are capable of in the next 5 years.

For deploying the A-29 Super Tucanos, rudimentary target marking methods such as colored smoke rounds put on target by mortars, as were sometimes used in World War II, could be made to work by the ANA—if they had trained forward air controllers (FACs), the necessary mortars and marking rounds in each unit, the tactical skill in each unit to put the marking rounds on the target, suitable communications equipment and training to enable ANA spotters on the ground to communicate with ANAF pilots, and if the ANAF had any aircraft capable of mounting weapons systems. As of December 2014, they do not have any of that. Assuming they could gain this capability rapidly with the four A-29s to be delivered in 2015 and put it into full operational use by the end of 2015, it would be entirely inadequate to the threat. As Giustozzi notes, "Neither the armed opposition nor Afghan Army troops on the ground are likely to be very impressed with these assets, having become accustomed to the mighty power of the USAF."[182]

During one period of particularly intense fighting around Sangin district in the late summer of 2014, for example, four Apache attack helicopters and an AC-130 Specter gunship were rotated continuously on station for nearly 2 days, with the Apaches completely expending their ordnance load-outs **eight times**.[183] The same scenario was repeated in the battle for the town of Sangar in Ajristan district of Ghazni province in late-September 2014. According to *The Los Angeles Times*, Afghan Commandos again had to be called in to prevent the town from being overrun by massed Taliban fighters conducting a "well-planned attack." Again, the commandos were backed by U.S. Apache helicopter gunships. "It was not pretty" said an Afghan NDS officer quoted by the *Times*, "just when we were about to collapse, at the last minute they sent in two foreign helicopters."[184] Anyone who has ever witnessed it knows that this represents a staggering concentration of sustained firepower. The little A-29s with their two wing-mounted machine guns, limited ammunition, and two small bombs or rockets (which have not yet been sourced) cannot begin to replace the heavier gunships.

The AC-130 Specter gunship, top, and A-10 Warthog, middle, lighting up targets. The Super Tucano light trainer, bottom, equipped with two machine guns and two rockets or bombs, is scheduled to replace them on the battlefield.

**Picture I-9. The AC-130 Specter Gunship, A-10 Warthog, and Super Tucano Trainer.**

At the same time, in practical terms, the ANA calling for CAS from U.S. military assets is, in soldier parlance, a "nonstarter." Afghans are not trained to do it; there is a huge language barrier; they do not have the communications equipment for it; for security reasons, we are not going to give it to them; and we do not even allow the U.S. Army to call for fire support directly from U.S. Navy and Marine Corps assets. (ANGLICO teams are attached to the U.S. Army for this purpose.[185]) Even then, there are tragic mistakes and deaths from friendly fire. Furthermore, there were far too many cases in the prosecution of the war in Afghanistan in which the United States was duped into conducting airstrikes aimed not at the Taliban, but at the informant's own personal enemies. The bottom line is that the only way the ANA is going to get U.S. CAS is if there are U.S. SF or SOF personnel on the ground with them to call for it. In this respect in particular, the failure to screen and vet ANA recruits adequately is coming home to roost at this stage of the war.[186] Because of the danger of green-on-blue attacks, this entails U.S. teams deploying only with reliable Afghan troops, such as the commando battalions.

Artillery and mortars in the hands of the ANA will not be a substitute for CAS. ANA use of artillery support was termed "dubious" by *Stars and Stripes* reporter Josh Smith in November 2014, who observed a 122-mm Soviet artillery piece being fired more or less at random toward a police operation a mile or two away. Major Eric Lightfoot, an artillery mentor, noted in January 2015 that the Afghans use a howitzer "sort of like a tank, for direct fire at enemies they [can] see."[187] The ANA mortaring of a village in Sangin district in January 2015, killing dozens of women and children at a wedding party, was typical of the ANA's indiscriminate use of fire support, according to Graeme Smith, the director of the International Crisis Group in Kabul. "I'm actually surprised that we haven't heard more complaints like this," Smith said:

> all of the anecdotal feedback is that ANSF have a very loose conception of the 'enemy' and uses artillery to blast locations they understand as 'Taliban villages.' My best guess is that civilian casualties frequently happen without complaints being registered, because the tribal groups associated with the insurgency don't feel they have any access to mechanisms of accountability.[188]

In November 2014, *The New York Times* revealed that President Obama signed a directive extending the U.S. combat role in Afghanistan through 2015. This was done in the wake of the Taliban campaign in Helmand province in the summer of 2014, in which it became clear that major Afghan government garrisons in the province would have been overrun without U.S.-supplied CAS. The presidential decision permits U.S. forces to assist the ANA by conducting air strikes, essentially by allowing them to perform both sides of the equation (requesting and delivering) through 2015.[189] The fact that the President of the United States was convinced that this step needed to be taken, at the political cost of abrogating his promise to the American public to end the U.S. combat role in Afghanistan at the end of 2014,[190] attests to the urgency of the lack of confidence of senior U.S. military leaders in the ability of the ANA to survive in 2015 without it. Indeed, the withdrawal of American close air support will be the beginning of the end for the ANA in the parts of southern and eastern Afghanistan where Pashtu is the predominant language.

# THE UNENDING CIVIL WAR

To see how these force capabilities will play out in the future of Afghanistan, it will be useful now to put the current situation in context, to zoom out to the 30,000-foot level, as it were, and examine the bigger picture. What is happening in Afghanistan today is not primarily a government vs. guerillas conflict. It is primarily a civil war. Afghanistan has been in a state of civil war, sometimes a cold war but most often a hot one, since 1973, more than 40 years. Entire library shelves are filled with academic treatises on the reasons for this conflict, and, to be certain, the reasons behind the conflict are as complex as the conflict itself. Almost anything one writes about Afghanistan runs the risk of being seen as too simplistic and reductionist. It is as if the English language itself is not nuanced enough to describe the intricately tangled web that is Afghanistan. There is, in fact, not one single war going on, but many interconnected ones, involving actors whose motivations run the gamut from religious fervor to mercenary gain, and these motivations are rarely pure or mutually exclusive.

There is a religious war, or holy war, taking place, that, on one level, is part of a cyclical pattern of Pashtun *jihad* in the region dating back centuries.[191] This element of the civil war in Afghanistan not only pits the Deobandi-inspired Taliban groups against the more moderate Hannafi Sunnis of the other ethnic groups and mixed communities of the north and east, it also pits the hard-line Sunnis of the Taliban against the ethnic minority Shi'a Hazara people of central Afghanistan. This kind of sectarian animus, whose intensity is being demonstrated so clearly in Iraq today, was already severe enough during the first period of

Taliban rule between 1996 and 2001 to provoke mass murders of the Hazara people and innumerable individual crimes against them across the Hazarajat by the Taliban during their reign.[192] The Hazaras, more so than any other ethnic group in Afghanistan, used the period of American engagement from 2001 to 2014 and the opportunities it offered to improve their traditional position as a permanent underclass in Afghan society. Despite deep-rooted discrimination and prejudice against them, for example, they are prominent in the army and at Kabul University.[193] Development programs in the Hazarajat were generally welcomed with open arms and experienced less of the subterfuge, security problems, and rampant corruption that plagued development efforts in the south. This refusal on the part of the Hazaras to accept their traditional underclass position in Afghan society has resulted in a backlash of resentment on the part of the other ethnic groups surrounding them. All four Hazaras nominated to ministerial posts by President Ghani were voted down by the Wolesi Jirga in January 2015. In military terms, these factors will intensify the violence against them and elevate future levels of retribution by the Taliban to the intensity being perpetrated against the Kurds and Yazidi and Shi'a populations by the ISIS terrorist group in Iraq and Syria today.

In addition to religious war, there is a constant struggle for Afghanistan's minimal wealth and resources among rival armed groups. These resources consist primarily of opium and increasingly profitable marijuana exports, but also include timber, semi-precious gems like lapis lazuli, and archeological relics, all of which are smuggled out relatively easily. Representations of the viability of Afghanistan's potential mineral wealth are often exaggerated: the extraction and marketing of such deep mineral deposits require not only a highly secure working environment, largely corruption-free civil and legal systems, and reliable land tenure; they also require a highly developed industrial infrastructure of paved roads and modern railways, huge amounts of electrical power and water, large-scale worker housing and sanitation, and very expensive deep extraction technologies and equipment, none of which Afghanistan has today or is going to have for decades.

Where there are no easily extractable resources such as opium, marijuana, timber, lapis lazuli, and cultural artifacts, the control of the border crossings themselves provides a major source of revenue from bribes, fees, and "taxes." Warlord militias and the various Taliban groups regularly contest these scant border revenue sources, often reaching local accords to divide the spoils, little of which ever reaches government coffers.[194]

Additionally, in Pashtun areas in particular, there are hundreds of ongoing feuds between clans like the Mashwari and the Salazai, many of which have resulted in false intelligence reports intended to bring about American military action against rivals. In the early years of the U.S.-Afghan war, the United States too easily fell victim to these scams, in one case in 2002 attacking the compound of a district governor in Uruzgan province allied with the United States and killing dozens of Afghan policemen and senior political leaders in hand-to-hand combat.[195] Many local feuds have been going on for decades, often preventing any kind of productive economic activity on the lands belonging to the warring families from perpetual fear of attacks by war parties and snipers. Some Pashtun clans, like the Mashwaris, Tanais, and Zadrans, do have long-standing animosity against tribes that support the Taliban, resulting in protracted local armed conflict between them, but, geographically and politically, they are few and far between. Frequently, several of these different types of conflicts overlap one another with an admixture of fighting motivations.

But by far the single greatest source of conflict in Afghan society is the millennium-old animosity between the Dari- and Uzbek-speaking northern ethnic groups and the Pashtu-speaking southern ethnic groups (including the Pashai[196]). Determining identity in Afghanistan, of course, is not as simplistic as many newly minted "cultural experts" employed by the military suggest.[197] In many cases, prevailing notions of ethnicity and identity in Afghanistan today were imported by the Americans themselves. Afghans in general do not identify themselves solely by a single ethnic label per se, any more than Americans do. Many communities are a mixture of villagers from different ethnic origins, often intermarried, and multilingualism is a part of day-to-day life.[198] Yet, broadly speaking, the political divide between Dari speakers and Pashtu speakers, often intertwined with disputes over land, water, religion, and resources, remains the largest obstacle to a sense of national identity and nation-building, a critical factor that will be discussed in detail in Part II.

It is this animus and chasm of trust between north and south, in general terms, that has driven the Afghan civil war since 1973 and will determine Afghanistan's fate in the next 5 years. The beginnings of the chaos and collapse of Afghan society which began 40 years ago can be traced directly to the bloodless overthrow of (Pashtun) Afghan King Zahir Shah by his cousin, Mohammed Daud, in 1973. Daud did not attempt to take the throne himself: rather, he seized power and attempted to rule the country without a king. The Afghan civil war began soon thereafter, and continues to this day. In Afghanistan, the existence of a king has not always been accompanied by peace, but the absence of a king has always been accompanied by war.

All of the events of the last 40 years in Afghanistan can be understood via this paradigm. The failed experiment with communism, which provoked Soviet intervention in 1979, was largely an outcome of a power struggle between the mostly Tajik *Parcham* faction and the predominantly Pashtun *Khalq* faction of the communist party of Afghanistan, the People's Democratic Party of Afghanistan (PDPA).[199] The PDPA split into these two main camps in 1967, but was still strong enough in 1973 to help Daud overthrow his cousin, King Zahir Shah. Daud's rule was brief, however. With help from the Afghan Army, the PDPA overthrew and killed Daud and his family in April 1978 in what is known as the Saur (April) Revolution, and established a communist government led by Ghilzai Pashtun Nur Mohammed Taraki and the *Khalq* faction.[200] In 1979, with the help of Soviet *Spetznaz* commandos, the *Parchami* faction overthrew the *Khalqi* faction and killed then (Ghilzai Pashtun) President Hafizullah Amin. The *Parchami* Tajik leader Babrak Karmal was installed as President.[201]

The PDPA, as subsequently reconciled by the Soviets, was supposed to be a government of national unity, with power shared between Pashtuns and Tajiks, but it remained deeply riven into these two ethnic power blocs. The PDPA began to implement unpopular reforms. It attempted to eliminate religion and carry out sweeping land reform in the rural areas in order to redistribute farmlands confiscated from the land-lord class to the feudal peasant farmers who worked them. These measures sparked an armed conservative backlash led by rural landowners and rural *mullahs* protecting their respective turfs, and for a variety of political economic reasons, the peasant sharecrop-ping farmers who stood to gain the most from land reform instead backed their landlords. The PDPA also attempted such equally radical social reforms in the 1970s such as allowing women to participate in pub-lic and political life, which shocked the conservative Afghan people.

The 10-year war that followed is commonly and wrongly presented as the "Soviet-Afghan" war, in which the Soviets are portrayed as fighting alone against heroic mujahideen fighters bravely repelling the invaders. The absurdly ahistorical 2007 Hollywood film *Charlie Wilson's War*, for example, is a classic of this genre.[202] Such myths are a part of every country's narrative, but the war was, in fact, nothing of the sort. In reality, the Soviets allied with a significant propor-tion of northern Afghans from the Tajik, Uzbek, and Hazara ethnic groups to fight the largely Pashtun mujahideen.

All major Afghan ethnicities (except the Shi'a Hazaras) were represented among the "Peshawar Seven," the seven mujahideen parties formed and recognized by the Pakistani Army via the Inter Ser-vices Intelligence Directorate (ISI), which armed them with weapons provided by the Central Intelligence Agency (CIA), and paid them with money provided by the intelligence service of Saudi Arabia.[203] Only Iran supported the Hazara resistance groups, under the umbrella of the *Hizb-e Wahdat-e Islami Afghanistan*.[204] In reality, however, the great bulk of the support (by ISI design) went to Pashtun groups, and actual resistance was largely carried out by Pashtuns (when they were not killing each other, a specialty of Gulbuddin Hekmatyar and his *Hizb-i-Islami Gulbuddin*, or HiG[205]). It was the Pashtuns who bore the brunt of the genocidal Soviet "drain-the-swamp" tactics.[206] The Soviets destroyed thousands of Pashtun villages and massacred as many as a million Pashtuns between 1979 and 1989.[207]

Of course, there were notable exceptions. The legendary Tajik mujahideen leader Ahmed Shah Masood, for example, was known as the "Lion of the Panshir."[208] Masood fought off countless Soviet offensives into the Panshir Valley north of the Soviet airbase at Bagram and subsequently led the last elements of resistance to the Taliban takeover of Afghanistan in 2001.[209]

Nevertheless, a large proportion of the fighting against the mujahideen was carried out by the conscript Afghan Army loyal to the PDPA and its Soviet advisors. Before the Soviet incursion, the (conscript) Afghan Army consisted of:

> . . . three armored divisions (570 medium tanks), eight infantry divisions (averaging 4,500 to 8,000 men each), two mountain infantry brigades, one artillery brigade, a guards regiment (for palace protection), three artillery regiments, two commando regiments, and a parachute battalion (largely grounded). All the formations were under the control of three corps level headquarters.[210]

After the Soviet occupation, significant parts of the Afghan Army deserted, but it remained in combat as an almost entirely Dari-speaking conscription force until the end of the war. Attrition through desertion was a constant problem, but it was never as high as the levels of desertion from the all-volunteer ANA today.[211] The communist Afghan Air Force was large

63

and capable, operating a variety of aircraft, including 240 fighter jets, among them three squadrons of MIG-21s. In fact, the current Commander of the ANAF, Lieutenant General Mohammad Dawran (a Tajik), flew against the mujahideen, compiling more than 2,000 cockpit hours in the MIG-21 and being trained as a cosmonaut by the Soviets.[212] Dispelling this mythos of the Soviet period as a "war of national liberation" is essential to understanding Afghanistan today in the context of the ongoing civil war. The Soviet period from 1979 to 1989 was, in fact, simply another chapter in the 40-year civil war between north and south.

After a protracted period of anarchy, characterized by an ethnic free-for-all, and created by ethnically based warlord armies vying for power following the Soviet withdrawal, the Taliban period from 1996 to 2001 was a continuation of the north-south civil war. The Taliban was, and is, a virtually 100 percent Pashtun movement, and resistance to it, apart from a handful of dissident Pashtun clans mentioned earlier, took the form of a Dari- and Uzbek-speaking resistance movement known as the Northern Alliance. It was comprised of Tajiks, Uzbeks, Hazaras, and Turkmen. The Northern Alliance gradually lost ground and retreated stubbornly in the face of the Pakistani Army-equipped and advised Taliban army. Pakistani advisors operated with the Taliban on the ground, and Pakistani Air Force pilots flew for the Taliban against the Northern Alliance.[213] The infamous "Operation Evil Airlift" out of Kunduz in November 2001, in which hundreds of senior Taliban and al-Qaeda leaders were airlifted out of the Kunduz Pocket to Peshawar in blacked-out Pakistani Air Force cargo aircraft under a secret agreement with the George W. Bush administration, was conducted as a face-saving measure for then-Pakistani President Pervez

Musharraf.[214] The airlift was intended to allow Musharraf to evacuate the hundreds of Pakistani Army advisors trapped in the Kunduz Pocket, and thus spare him the international embarrassment of revealing the Pakistani Army's blatant role in supporting and supplying the Taliban.[215] The ISI naturally used the opportunity to get its Afghan Taliban and al-Qaeda leadership out at the same time.[216] In fact, the Taliban, then as today, operates as a de facto expeditionary division of the Pakistan Army, run by the army's intelligence branch, the ISI.[217]

The two primary points here are that the various military groups comprising the Taliban, including the Quetta Shura group, the Haqqani Network, HiG, the Tora Bora front, *Hizb-i-Islami Khalis*, and others, are almost 100 percent ethnically Pashtuns, and that the Afghan Taliban, the Haqqani Network, HiG, and so on were, and are, a de facto extension of the Pakistani Army that is trained, equipped, supplied, advised, and given refuge and medical care by the Pakistani government, as Admiral Mike Mullen noted in 2011.[218] The rationale for this on the part of Pakistan remains Pakistan's strategic shibboleth, "security in depth," which requires Pakistan to maintain proxy control over Afghanistan in order to keep India off of its northern flank and avoid its psychological *bête noir*, a hypothetical two-front war with India.[219] Some observers interpret the ongoing war in Afghanistan almost exclusively as an extension of this dynamic. "Fundamentally, the war in Afghanistan is an Indo-Pakistan proxy conflict layered atop Afghanistan's ethnic cleavages," Thomas Lynch of the National Defense University's Institute for National Strategic Studies has argued. "In this decades-old struggle, NATO counterinsurgency forces are but a temporary participant."[220]

In 2001, following the attacks of September 11, the United States allied itself with the Northern Alliance and stepped into this ongoing north-south civil war, either without comprehending this context or ignoring it. The reemergence of the Taliban in late-2002, in the form of an incipient insurgency,[221] its rise from the ashes to control large swathes of rural Afghanistan, the power struggles within the kleptocratic Karzai administration,[222] the recent electoral conflict between the Pashtun Ashraf Ghani and the Tajik Abdullah Abdullah,[223] and the 4-month delay in even nominating a cabinet are all further manifestations of this civil war. Now that the United States is departing Afghanistan, it is once again heating up. Taliban attacks spiked in 2014, and the largely Tajik Afghan National Army and the locally recruited Afghan National Police both suffered casualties that reached record highs during the year.[224]

Ashraf Ghani, who was pronounced the winner despite "industrial-scale" electoral fraud,[225] actually has very little overall support among the people.[226] Barely a third of eligible voters cast legitimate ballots in the two elections of 2014, meaning that, at best, Ghani has the active support of one-half of one-third of the population, or perhaps 18 percent, since the outcome of the voting was presented as a nearly 50-50 split.[227] According to surveys conducted by the Asia Foundation in 2013, the Taliban has the support of approximately a third of the Afghan people today.[228]

Thus approximately one-third of the Afghan people cared enough to vote for one candidate or the other in the elections of 2014, one-third support the Taliban, and one-third simply want to be left alone or are entirely apathetic to their future.

| AFGHAN COMMUNIST ARMY | | | |
|---|---|---|---|
| YEAR | ARMY | AIR FORCE | PARAMIL |
| 1978 | 80-90,000 | 10,000 | |
| 1979 | 50-100,000 | 5,000 | |
| 1980 | 20-25,000 | | |
| 1981 | 25-35,000 | | |
| 1982 | 25-40,000 | | |
| 1983 | 35-40,000 | 5-7,000 | |
| 1984 | 35-40,000 | | |
| 1985 | 35-40,000 | 7,000 | 50,000 |
| 1986 | 40,000 | | 60,000 |
| 1987 | | | 70,000 |
| 1988 | | | 80,000 |
| 1989 | | | 100,000 |

Numbers are incomplete but some may be extropolated. In the final years of the war, the Soviets also attempted to raise irregular units like the ALP. The Soviets also had trouble with "green on red" attacks, and came to rely heavily on the Afghan Commando Brigades (444th, 37th, and 38th) toward the end of the war, just as U.S. SF and SOF rely heavily on them today. Attrition from the all-conscript communist army was lower than that of the ANA today.

**Figure 1. PDPA Force Size from 1978 to 1989.**

In other words, of the one-third who cared enough to vote in 2014, roughly half supported President Ashraf Ghani, the great majority of them being Pashtuns. The Afghan government today, a shotgun marriage of north and south following the bitterly contested election audit process, is an extra-constitutional "government of national unity" in which the fault lines between Ghani's supporters among the anti-Taliban Pashtun, including many former Khalkis like Mohammed Afzal Lodin[229] and Shah Nawaz Tanai,[230] and the Tajik supporters of Abdullah Abdullah, who include the second most powerful man in Afghanistan, Mohammed Atta,[231] are already beginning to appear.[232] Today's "government of national unity" cobbled together by the United States not only resembles the PDPA "government of national unity" cobbled together by the Soviet Union in 1979, but it also features many of the same cast of characters. The new Minster of the Interior, for example, Nur ul-Haq Ulumi, was a Parcham member of the PDPA.[233] Only a third of the "government of national unity" ministerial choices were accepted by the Wolesi Jirga.[234] Meanwhile, apparently not fully grasping the Afghan Constitution's prohibition of elected leaders having private militias, First Vice President of Afghanistan and former PDPA officer Rashid Dostum[235] spent the month of December 2014 resurrecting his private 20,000-man *Junbish* (Uzbek) militia to "root out Taliban" from Kunduz province.[236]

Former communist party members are prominent among Ghani supporters. Khalqi general Mohammed Afzal Lodin, left, is a leading Ghani supporter and was briefly his nominee for Minister of Defense. Shah Nawaz Tanai of Khost province, center (seen here wearing his Khalqi general's uniform in his 2014 presidential campaign poster) was the Chief of Staff of the Army under Najibullah. Nur ul-Haq Ulumi, right, former prominent Parchami faction member and Lieutenant General in the communist army, is now the Minister of the Interior.

**Picture I-10. Ghani Supporters Mohammed Afzal Lodia, Shah Nawaz Tanai, and Nur ul-Haq Ulumi.**

## ATTRITION: THE FORCE KILLER

Returning now to the Afghan security forces, having situated them within this broader context of the ongoing ethnic civil war, what follows is an explication of their operational problems. The first of these are force size, force maturity, combat experience, and attrition.

National Military Training Center-Afghanistan (NMTC-A)/Combined Security Transition Command-Afghanistan (CSTC-A) deliberately obscured these statistics for years by reporting only the "trained and equipped" numbers and refusing to share the statistics with the State Department and other government agencies.[237] According to SIGAR, the reported strength of the ANA as of January 2014 was 149,185 men, not counting civilians and "Trainee, Transient, Holdee, and Student" numbers.[238] In a rare moment of ISAF candor, on December 11, 2014, Lieutenant General Anderson told *Reuters* news agency that 20 percent of the 195,000 authorized ANA billets are currently unfilled because "recruiting and retention aren't matching, and, of course, don't forget losses," indicating a total strength in December 2014 of 156,000 men, including the approximately 6,000 personnel of the ANAF.[239] This number tallies with the first quarter 2014 SIGAR report figure (149,185, **not** including the ANAF) and may be considered reliable.

According to U.S. Government figures, during the 12-month period of September 2012 to September 2013, the ANA lost 67,682 men to attrition. British government figures are comparable. As reported by *The Independent* in 2013:

the latest British Government assessments . . . confirm that the rate of recruits leaving is far worse than targets set by coalition leaders, amounting to 63,000 every year, or more than a third of the current size of the army.[240]

Using SIGAR's 2014 figures of 149,185 men actually wearing uniforms and on the rosters,[241] the loss of 67,682 men in a year to desertion represents 45 percent of the entire army. The ANA recruited only 64,383 new soldiers during the same period.[242] Only about 54,000 of them made it through the mild basic training course, because the basic training dropout rate is 16 percent.[243] Thus, the ANA lost some 13,600 more men than it could recruit in the year between September 2012 and September 2013. (In comparison, the all-conscript ARVN suffered 20 percent attrition in 1973,[244] and the all-conscript Afghan Army fighting with the Soviets against the mujahideen never had more than 35 percent attrition.[245]) Recruiting statistics are hard to come by and are now classified, but there were several months in 2013 in which the ANA did not meet its recruiting goals,[246] and Lieutenant General Anderson's observations on December 11, 2014, indicate a 20 percent recruiting shortfall in 2014.[247] This suggests that not only has the number of recruits which can be found annually reached its maximum level and is starting to decline (in a country with 50 percent unemployment[248]), but also that the maximum recruiting level is now below the current level of annual attrition, and the ANA is shrinking. At a minimum, what can be said with certainty is that the ANA has reached its maximum possible size at roughly 150,000 men.

In point of fact, no one knows exactly how many soldiers and policemen are actually present for duty on any given day. The precise figures given lend a false sense of credibility and confidence in numbers which are, in actuality, mostly estimates. Personnel accountability in the ANSF, and in the police in particular, is in its infancy. ISAF is almost entirely reliant on Ministry of Defense (MOD) and MOI reports of force size, so, although the United States pays the salaries of every soldier and policeman the MOD and MOI say are present, we do not have any granularity on ANSF numbers because western personnel literally never count them. As the DoD Inspector General reported in August 2014:

> the [government of Afghanistan] lacked the basic controls to provide reasonable assurance that it appropriately spent $3.3 billion of ASFF [Afghan Security Forces Fund] direct contributions. . . . As a result of [the government of Afghanistan's] internal control weaknesses, CSTC-A cannot verify that the ASFF direct contributions were properly spent or used for their intended purposes.[249]

SIGAR added in 2013 that:

> Determining ANSF strength is fraught with challenges. U.S. and coalition forces rely on the Afghan forces to report their own personnel strength numbers. Moreover, the . . . CSTC-A noted that, in the case of the [ANA], there is 'no viable method of validating [their] personnel numbers'.[250]

Unlike western armies, Afghan soldiers and policemen routinely "self-transfer" to other units for personal and ethnic reasons. Maintaining "ghost soldiers" on the rolls is an entrenched Afghan military tradition that allows commanders to report imaginary men in order to receive extra bulk rations that are sold on the grey market to supplement their meager officer salaries. In December 2014, it was reported that the Iraqi government of Prime Minister Haidar al-Abadi had discovered the presence of 50,000 such "ghost soldiers" on the roles of the Iraqi Army as well.[251] Giustozzi notes that payment of ANA salaries by electronic funds transfers and the presence of U.S. combat advisors kept a lid on ghost soldiering in the ANA, but with the advisors now gone, there are no formal structures within the ANA to prevent it from increasing.[252]

Behind the smoke and mirrors surrounding the doctrinally already inadequate 149,185 ANA force size number cited by SIGAR and Lieutenant General Anderson (not counting the 6,000 man air force),[253] the reality is sobering. Of the reported total "assigned strength" of the ANA of 149,185, only 119,485 men are designated as combat-assigned troops (the six Corps commands, the Commandos, and the Kabul 111 [static garrison and parade] Division). The remaining 30,000 are rear area staff and headquarters personnel. Of this 119,485, SIGAR found that a further 9,000 men who were still on the books and counted as "assigned" were actually deserters not yet removed from the rolls, another 15,915 were **still in basic training** or on administrative hold,[254] and 9,236 were civilians.[255] Thus 34,151 men "assigned" to the combat forces were not in them, or were not even soldiers — almost 30 percent. This does not include men on authorized leave.

To determine the "not present plus authorized leave" number and calculate the actual fighting strength of the ANA, SIGAR's statistics from the previous 12 months can be used. SIGAR found at the beginning of 2012 that out of the (then) strength of the ANA on paper of 176,354, only **63 percent** were actually present for duty.[256] Thus the "not present" plus "authorized leave" number equals roughly 37 percent of the assigned number.

Using this statistic of 37 percent as an approximate relative constant, of the 119,485 who were assigned to combat commands in December 2014 (the six ANA Army Corps, the 111th Capital Division, and the commandos) only **75,258 soldiers were actually in fighting units and present for duty**.[257] This is the real fighting strength of the ANA. Only **41 percent** of the big ANA number are actual soldiers actually present in combat units. In other words, cutting through the smoke and mirrors, SIGAR found that ISAF was routinely counting deserters, civilians, recruits in basic training, the sick, the halt, the lame, the wounded, men on leave, and rear echelon clerks and generals as "trained and equipped" or "assigned" to make the end strength number appear larger, the ANA appear more ready, and the ANA program appear more successful.[258] The reality is that, in all of Afghanistan, there are only about 75,000 soldiers actually out there with guns in their hands, or one for every 3.4 square miles of the country. The comparable actual fighting strength of the police in the field is 53,500.

In addition, despite the bar being constantly lowered by ISAF for this metric,[259] there are still only a handful of ANA battalions rated as being able to operate entirely without U.S. advisors or support.[260] In April, 2013, a force of over 200 Taliban attacked one of them, the Third Battalion, Second Brigade, 201 Corps, in Nari district of Kunar province, wiped out the entire garrison of 13 men, and captured the outpost.[261] In contrast, from 1971 on, the entire ARVN operated without U.S. advisors or support. At the time of publication, the extent of possible future analysis of the ANA personnel situation is unclear, because while Operation RESOLUTE SUPPORT is walking back its much-criticized[262] unilateral[263] decision to classify ANA personnel and readiness numbers,[264] which data will remain classified is still unknown. If the numbers were good, however, it seems unlikely they would been classified in the first place after 6 years of open publication.

Moreover, attrition is not constant across the force. It is understandably much higher in combat units in the south than in comfortable rear area staff positions in major cities, or in corps in the north that are not regularly engaged in fighting. Attrition from the 205 Corps operating in Kandahar, Uruzgan, and Daykundi provinces in 2014 was 42 percent.[265] In the summer of 2014, the 2nd Brigade of the ANA's 215 Corps operating in northern Helmand suffered 70 percent attrition.[266] (The U.S. Army rates a unit as "combat ineffective" when its personnel strength declines to 50 percent.[267]) In 2014, there were approximately 25,500 men in these two Corps (205 and 215), and about 13,000 of them deserted. In contrast, the highest rate of attrition experienced by the conscript Afghan Army fighting with the Soviets against the mujahideen was about 35 percent,[268] while attrition from the conscript ARVN in 1973 was about 20 percent.[269] Thus, the all-volunteer ANA has double the desertion rate of the all-conscript ARVN, not a good indicator of its fighting spirit. In short, the combat element of the ANA is about 75,258 men, fully half of whom have been in the army less than 12 months. How would U.S. Army officers evaluate the U.S. Army if half of it deserted every year and half of the remainder had been in the Army less than 12 months?

Casualties, another source of attrition, have also risen alarmingly. Approximately 4,000 ANA soldiers have been killed in action in the last 34 months.[270] In fact, casualties are at an all-time high and rising.[271] Lieutenant General Anderson described these casualty figures in November 2014 as "not sustainable," noting that the ANSF (Army and Police) have suffered 9,000 KIA since the beginning of 2013.[272] In 2012, 1,170 ANA soldiers were killed in action or died of their wounds,[273] by 2013 the number had risen to 1,400 soldiers,[274] and in the first 6 months of 2014, approximately 950 soldiers died.[275] (Almost 3,000 ANP personnel were killed in 2013 alone, and some 3,500 died in the first 10 months of 2014.[276]) The numbers of ANSF personnel wounded in action (WIA) and no longer present for duty are very difficult to acquire; apparently the ANA and ANP either do not keep close records of the numbers of personnel wounded or do not regularly release them to the public. In February 2013, the Watson Institute for International Studies at Brown University put the number of Afghan military and police WIA at 30,471, "estimated using the common ratio for other conflicts of three soldiers wounded for every one killed."[277]

Using this formula, in addition to 4,000 ANA soldiers KIA in the previous 34 months, another 12,000 have been WIA. SIGAR reported that between March 2012 and February 2014, the ANA had 2,166 personnel KIA and 11,804 WIA, an actual wounded-to-killed ratio of 5.4-to-1, so the common 3:1 ratio may be much too low.[278] Using the SIGAR 5.4-to-1 ratio as a relative constant and Lieutenant General Anderson's figures, in addition to 9,000 overall ANSF KIA since the beginning of 2013, another 48,600 have been wounded.[279] Some 57,600 combat casualties (KIA plus WIA) in 2 years, not counting missing in action (MIAs) and prisoners of war (POWs) or losses from disease and noncombat related injuries, represents almost 45 percent of the entire present-for-duty combat fighting strength of the ANSF of 128,500, a staggering statistic. (In comparison, in the 4 years of World War II, 6 percent of all Americans who served in uniform were killed or wounded.[280]) Perhaps most importantly from a strategic viewpoint, during 2013, the Taliban suffered an estimated 10,000 to 12,000 men killed, wounded, and captured. During the same period, ANSF casualties (ANA plus ANP killed and wounded) were 20,960. In other words, in 2013, Afghan government security forces suffered two casualties for every one they inflicted on the enemy.[281]

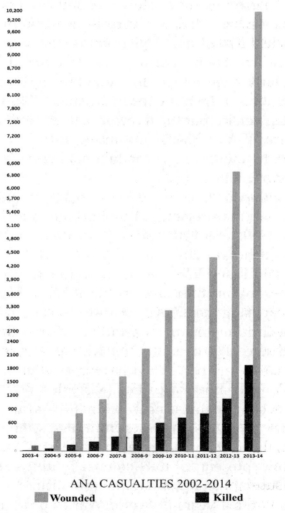

ANA CASUALTIES 2002-2014

Wounded      Killed

## Figure 2. ANA Casualties from 2002 to 2014.

## THE ETHNIC TIME BOMB

The ANA has one other major, largely hidden problem that is not often discussed, at least not publicly: It is largely a Northern Alliance army. The danger is that the heavily Tajik ANA is being portrayed by the Taliban as "an occupying power in the south," as U.S. Senator Lindsey Graham (Republican, South Carolina) noted in June 2014.[282] A similar dynamic was in play when the Sunni terrorist group known as ISIS attacked Mosul. The Shia-dominated Iraqi Army in Mosul abandoned the city rapidly in June 2014.[283]

Statistical analysis proves conclusively that the routinely presented ANA ethnic balance numbers simply are not accurate. The boilerplate numbers of approximately 43 percent Pashtuns and 35 percent Tajiks coincide precisely with what is known as the "Eikenberry Rule,"[284] guidelines promulgated by Lieutenant General Karl Eikenberry during his first tour in Afghanistan from September 2002 to September 2003, when he served as both the U.S. Security Coordinator for Afghanistan and as Chief of the Office of Military Cooperation-Afghanistan.[285] The Eikenberry Rule stipulates that the ethnic mix of the ANA will closely mirror that of Afghan society, so that it will not be perceived as the army of one or the other of the country's major ethnic groups so that it will serve as a symbol of national unity.[286] In fact, the reported ethnic mix of the ANA today is, astonishingly, a **perfect** mirror of Afghan society that precisely reflects the Eikenberry Rule — not close, or somewhat imbalanced, as is, for example, the U.S. Army, but **perfect**.

However, this is not only *ipso facto* suspicious, but there is substantial anecdotal and statistical evidence that it is not true. The Pashtun presence in the ANA is being exaggerated, and to understand how, some understanding of the ethnic group is necessary. The Pashtuns in Afghanistan are not one monolithic people, but a large, segmentary descent group comprising more than 350 major independent tribes,[287] each one, in a strictly demographic, organizational sense, roughly analogous to a Native American tribe such as the Apache, Navajo, Sioux, Comanche, and so on. Determining who is a Pashtun and who is not is not always simple: some Pashtuns pretend they are not and speak Dari, while some clans are not ethnically Pashtun but speak Pashto and claim to be Pashtun.

In general terms, the Pashtuns are classified by academic experts into four major tribal groups that have a substantial presence in Afghanistan, and a fifth group that lives almost entirely in Pakistan.[288] The "Eastern Pashtuns" of Afghanistan live in the area around Jalalabad and are comprised of scores of tribes known collectively as the *Sarbani* as a result of their ancestral claims.[289] Former Afghan President Hamid Karzai is from the "Western Pashtun" tribal group, known to ethnographers as the *Durrani* or *Abdali* group. The kings of Afghanistan and their courts were virtually all descended from this tribal group. They reside primarily in the area around Kandahar. In the same southern region are found the third tribal grouping, the *Ghilzai* or *Bitani* group,[290] traditional rivals of the *Durranis*. The deepest rivalry among the *Ghilzai* is between the two major tribes, the *Hotaki* and the *Ahmadzai*. Taliban founder *Mullah* Omar is from the *Hotaki* tribe, and Afghan president Ashraf Ghani Ahmadzai is from the *Ahmadzai* tribe.[291] Much of the original inner core element of the original Taliban movement were *Hotakis*.[292] Afghan president Ashraf Ghani Ahmadzai draws his support base from among the *Ahmadzais*, including many former members of the *Khalq* faction of the PDPA. The U.S. military erroneously aggregates these two tribal groups together under the rubric of the "Southern Pashtuns," a spurious classification that has no ethnographic basis or academic validity beyond a broad geographic description of where they live.

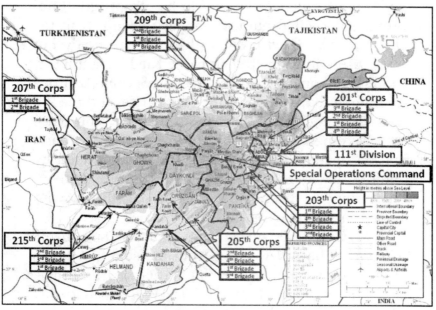

Source: Map courtesy of The Long War Journal.

**Map I-2. ANA Corps Commands.**

The fourth major tribal grouping are the *Karlanri* (putatively descended from another son of the *ur*-ancestor of the Pashtuns[293] named Karlan[294]). They are referred to often as the "hill tribes," the rough mountain men and women who most closely hold to the old tribal traditions and laws. They live in the inhospitable and often barren mountains of south-central Afghanistan. Many of them live across the largely imaginary Durand Line in the tribal areas of northern Pakistan (the Federally Administered Tribal Areas). The *Karlanri* are the Appalachian mountaineers of Afghanistan—

they avoid all contact with any government, Afghan or Pakistani. For this reason, virtually none of them may be found in the ranks of the ANA, although some served as scouts in former British times in irregular formations like the Khyber Rifles.[295]

In rough terms, the Pashtun population of Afghanistan then could be said to be comprised of approximately equal numbers of each group, with the *Durrani* and *Ghilzai* groups (the latter generally but not entirely includes the nomadic Kuchi Pashtuns[296]) comprising some 25 percent each, the *Sarbani* Pashtuns forming perhaps 30 percent of the whole, and the hill tribes making up roughly another 20 percent. Since they have never been counted, these are only rough but reasonable estimates based on data collected by Louis Adamec, Louis Dupree, and Henry Priestly.[297] This is important because it is critical to getting at who among them are in the ANA.

NMTC-A/CTSC-A statistics indicate that only 3 percent of the ANA comes from the southern provinces inhabited by the *Durrani* and *Ghilzai* Pashtuns, i.e., "southern Pashtuns."[298] *The Wall Street Journal* reported in September 2010 that:

> southern Pashtuns accounted for . . . 1.1 percent [of ANA recruits] in July [2010] and 1.8 percent in August [2010]. Last month [August 2010], just 66 of the 3,708 Afghan recruits were Pashtuns, U.S. officials said.[299]

This is not surprising: The *Durrani* historically have never participated in any Afghan army; almost in the social sense that the once-rigid caste system in India determined which occupation a given caste would perform, the *Durrani* did not enter military service. Correspondingly, as much of the support for the Taliban comes from the *Ghilzai* tribes, their formerly-strong participation in the old royal Afghan Army of the 1960s can now be expected to be rather low. In the king's time, the Afghan Army officer corps was the sinecure of the *Ghilzai*,[300] who have a traditional reputation as fighters, but that is no longer the case.

Since the *Karlanri* generally do not participate in any government institutions, including the police or the army, in any statistically meaningful numbers[301] and the misnomered Southern Pashtuns (the *Durrani* and *Ghilzai* tribal groups) are providing only 3 percent of the force according to NMTC-A statistics,[302] this requires, mathematically, that the Eastern or *Sarbani* Pashtuns are supplying 40 percent of the ANA.[303] This is, at best, dubious. Nangarhar has been the most fertile recruiting ground for the ANA since its inception,[304] but the contention that two of four major tribal groups (the *Durrani* and *Ghilzai* groups) are together providing 3 percent,[305] the third group (the *Karlanri*) are essentially providing none, and the fourth (the Eastern, or *Sarbani* Pashtuns), who comprise roughly 12 percent of the overall Afghan population, would therefore be providing 40 percent of the entire army would require credulity bordering on a "suspension of disbelief."[306]

Instead, to increase the numbers, ISAF decided in 2006 to include so-called "northern Pashtuns."[307] This demographic segment of Afghan society is theoretically comprised of the detribalized descendants of several tens of thousands of Pashtuns forced to leave their homes more than a century ago by Abdul Rahman Khan, the ruler of Afghanistan from 1880 to 1901.[308] Mostly intermixed and intermarried with northern ethnic groups for more than 100 years, most of these people today are only Pashtuns in a narrow genealogical sense. In many cases, they no longer speak Pashto. However, testifying before the Defense

Committee of the House of Commons, *Evening Standard* defense correspondent Robert Fox reported in 2013 that "the disproportionate element [of the ANA] among the Pashtuns are the northern Pashtuns."[309]

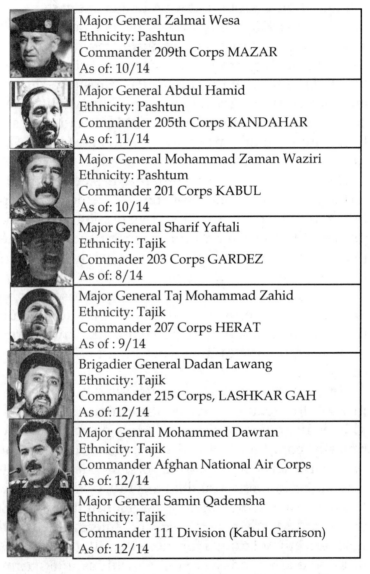

| | |
|---|---|
| | Major General Zalmai Wesa<br>Ethnicity: Pashtun<br>Commander 209th Corps MAZAR<br>As of: 10/14 |
| | Major General Abdul Hamid<br>Ethnicity: Pashtun<br>Commander 205th Corps KANDAHAR<br>As of: 11/14 |
| | Major General Mohammad Zaman Waziri<br>Ethnicity: Pashtum<br>Commander 201 Corps KABUL<br>As of: 10/14 |
| | Major General Sharif Yaftali<br>Ethnicity: Tajik<br>Commader 203 Corps GARDEZ<br>As of: 8/14 |
| | Major General Taj Mohammad Zahid<br>Ethnicity: Tajik<br>Commander 207 Corps HERAT<br>As of : 9/14 |
| | Brigadier General Dadan Lawang<br>Ethnicity: Tajik<br>Commander 215 Corps, LASHKAR GAH<br>As of: 12/14 |
| | Major Genral Mohammed Dawran<br>Ethnicity: Tajik<br>Commander Afghan National Air Corps<br>As of: 12/14 |
| | Major General Samin Qademsha<br>Ethnicity: Tajik<br>Commander 111 Division (Kabul Garrison)<br>As of: 12/14 |

**Picture I-11. Ethnicities of Afghan Commanders.**

More importantly, in terms of actual numbers, many Afghans of Pashtun and mixed-Pashtun heritage in the north were persecuted for their Pashtun roots despite the fact that they had almost unanimously allied themselves with their Northern Alliance neighbors in 2001 following the fall of the Taliban (another ugly dimension of the ongoing civil war).[310] In the face of coercive ethnic cleansing, many fled to the south and to Pakistan refugee camps in the following years. This flood of refugees left behind a very small military recruiting pool. Furthermore, the entire fighting age male population of this invented ethnic group remaining in northern Afghanistan in 2014 is likely smaller than the entire ANA today. Most critically, after their persecution beginning in 2002, few feel any affinity any longer for their former Northern Alliance allies and are more likely to be aiding the Taliban in the north than fighting them.[311] As Brookings Institute noted in 2011, "The Taliban has been rather effectively mobilizing among the northern Pashtuns who feel discriminated by Tajiks."[312] As a result, there are probably more Turkmen in Afghanistan and more Turkmen in the Afghan National Army today than so-called Northern Pashtuns. Counting them as Pashtuns in the ANA is intellectually dishonest at best; counting them as being in large numbers in the ANA is plain dishonest.

In fact, there is substantial anecdotal evidence that Pashtuns comprise only a small fraction of the ANA, and the Eikenberry Rule is a fig leaf that remains in place for propaganda purposes. Ben Anderson, who has been reporting on the ANA for nearly a decade, reported in 2013 that "It's an exaggeration to call this a national army. It's not. It's the Northern Alliance." Noting the photos of Masood and Dostum taped in most of the ANA vehicle windows in Helmand province, Anderson says, "These guys look almost as foreign to the Pashtuns as we do."[313] Former British Ambassador Craig Murray recounts a conversation with a senior British officer in the CTSC-A program in 2010 as saying the ANA is now over 60 percent Tajik. "The Pashtun figure is hovering below 20 percent and may have been overtaken by the Uzbeks," according to Ambassador Murray.[314] Indeed, a substantial number of Hazaras have also joined the army as a way out of the menial labor jobs most often open to them in Afghan society. Visual evidence corroborates this. The author saw many Hazaras but few Pashtuns in the *Kandaks* operating in Paktika province during his service in Afghanistan. In fact, Tajiks, Uzbeks, Hazaras, and Pashtuns are usually quite easy to distinguish from one another for an experienced observer (any Afghan recognizes it instantly), and in photos and videos of the ANA, it is difficult to spot a Pashtun in the ranks.[315] On an operation in April 2012, CNN observed the "Afghan soldiers [were] mostly from the north or northeast of Afghanistan."[316] In 2011 NBC News reported:

> The Afghan army tries to ensure a mix of ethnic groups in each brigade of enlisted soldiers, but it is hard to find a brigade that northerners do not dominate. Of the nearly 40 soldiers based with the Americans at Combat Outpost Ware in the Arghandab Valley, only two are Pashtun. One of them is the cook.[317]

Tajiks are heavily over-represented in the officer ranks as well, especially in operational billets, such as corps commanders. Of the eight most important operational billets, the six regional corps commands, the ANAF Chief of Staff[318] (designated as a corps), and the 111th (Capital) Division, five are held by Tajiks.[319] That represents approximately 63 percent of the top operational commands — almost exactly double their proportion of the Afghan population. During his tenure as Minister of Defense, Bismullah Khan packed the mid- and senior-level officer ranks with Tajiks.[320] How can the Pashtuns be 43 percent of the army when it is hard to find one in the ranks? As Arthur Conan Doyle's famous character Sherlock Holmes often noted, "Once you eliminate the impossible, whatever remains, no matter how improbable, must be the truth."[321] The deduction here is obvious: Tajik officers in the MOD mid-levels charged with producing the ethnic balance numbers in accordance with the Eikenberry Rule to maintain foreign funding are simply falsifying the numbers.

In reality, an educated, well-informed estimate of the representation of Pashtuns in the ANA in early-2015 would be no greater than 15 percent, comprised of roughly 3 percent southern Pashtuns as reported by NMTC-A, 10 percent eastern Pashtuns (approximately equal to their representation in the general population), and 2 percent northern Pashtuns, Afghans of Pashtun descent born in Pakistani refugee camps, and Pashai.

## THE ELEPHANT IN THE ROOM

The problems of small force size, over-reliance on weak police forces at this late stage of the insurgency, limited mobility, lack of organic CAS and indirect fire support, a virtually nonexistent logistics capability, 40 percent annual ANA attrition and 50 percent annual ANP attrition, and severe ethnic imbalance in the ANA are only the most significant of ANSF operational problems. There is also, for example, a major and growing problem of drug use and drug addiction in both the ANA and the ANP. SIGAR reported the number of ANA soldiers using drugs was "at least 50 percent," while the figure regularly cited is 75 percent,[322] and it may be as high as 85 percent of all Afghan soldiers, according to some reports.[323] As Paul Lacapruccia, who worked on the Border Management Task Force training Afghan border guards at Torkham Gate in 2014, noted: "Afghanistan has hundreds of thousands of armed, uniformed service members who are paid with our aid money. Most of them are illiterate drug addicts. I know. I trained them."[324] A video entitled "The Hashish Army — The Afghan National Army" showing an entire ANA unit high on drugs was popular on *YouTube* in 2009.[325] A similar hour-long film by *Vice News* entitled "This is What Winning Looks Like" showing pervasive ANA and ANP drug use was put online in 2013.[326]

The real strategic impediment, however, and the elephant in the room, is the inability of the Afghan government to come close to being able to sustain its security forces without international financial donations of some $4.1 billion annually.[327] Only $500 million of the annual costs, or roughly 12 percent, is to be provided by the Afghan government.[328] According to World Bank statistics, Afghan government revenues have been declining steadily since 2011.[329] The World Bank reported in December 2014 that Afghan economic growth "collapsed from an average 9.4 percent growth between 2003-2012 to 1.5 percent this year."[330] As the civil war in Afghanistan increases in intensity, further reducing Afghanistan's already limited appeal to foreign investors, revenue-producing foreign presence and investment will decrease further. Afghan government revenues will thus continue to decline, not increase. Afghanistan's public revenue for 2014 is projected to be U.S.$2.4 billion—half the cost of the ANSF alone.[331]

In meetings with the author in Kabul beginning in 2001, successive Afghan Ministers of Defense Mohammed Fahim, Rahim Wardak, Bismullah Khan, and the recently nominated and Sandhurst-educated Sher Mohammed Karimi (as of February 2015 the Chief of Staff of the ANA), all impressed upon me the unsustainability of the all-volunteer force structure of the ANA on which U.S. Army leaders insisted. All previous Afghan armies in history had been conscript armies.[332] This was the Afghan way of making armies, and of making them ethnically balanced. "How will we pay for this when you're gone?" Rahim Wardak asked me in 2002.[333] He and other Afghan military leaders knew full well that a professional western-style army would be prohibitively expensive to pay and maintain, and urged our delegation to utilize conscription instead. They agreed unanimously that when U.S. funding eventually ceased, the Afghan government would be forced to switch over to a system of conscription as their only option, and so it may well prove to be. In the meantime, they were content to get what they could in terms of military resources from the United States.

It is unclear what sober and reasoned judgment led the U.S. Army to build an unsustainable, high-tech, and very expensive professional army in its own image in Afghanistan, despite all the polite advice of Afghan military leaders with decades of professional experience operating in one of the most impoverished countries in the world,[334] but it was a poor one. Former Special Forces officer Kalev Sepp conducted a seminal study on best practices in counterinsurgency over the previous 50 years, identifying commonalities of success and failure. High on the list in every failed counterinsurgency is "building [and] training indigenous army in [the] image of U.S. Army."[335]

In simple terms, Afghanistan cannot begin to afford its own army today, and even under the most optimistic economic projections for the Afghan economy, it would not be able to do so for decades.[336] Events of the next 5 years, however, will render this a moot point.

## COUNTERVAILING ARGUMENTS

The most obvious counterargument to the comparison of the fates of the ARVN in Vietnam and the ANA in Afghanistan is that the Taliban does not have tanks, and they are not the regular North Vietnamese Army (NVA) with major backing from the Soviet Union and China. The Taliban are irregulars, it is argued, not a conventional force like the NVA, nor can their numbers begin to approach the strength of the NVA. This is true, as far as it goes, but by the same token the ANA is not the ARVN either, and if the NVA was 15 times more powerful than the Taliban, the ARVN was at least 15 times more powerful than the ANA, while suffering half the attrition from desertions and having a quarter of the terrain to defend. The relative size comparison is, in fact, quite good. The NVA had the backing of the nuclear-armed Soviet Union and nuclear-armed China; the Afghan Taliban, Haqqani Network, HiG, HiK (Hizb-i Islami Khalis), Tora Bora Front, and other *jihadi* groups have the backing of nuclear-armed Pakistan. The Taliban may not have tanks, but for all intents and purposes, neither does the ANA. Within the 111th Division of the ANA, there is a single tank battalion equipped with 44 T-55 and T-62 tanks. Half of them, however, are "hangar queens," vehicles used for spare parts, and only about 20 can actually run. All are in poor repair; none are less than 40 years old, there are no tank transporters, and the road distance any of them could travel without breaking down is questionable. Ammunition for the main guns is scarce, as are tankers who know how to operate them. Most importantly, there is no concept of combined arms and the use of armor in conjunction with infantry and artillery in the ANA, let alone any training or experience. Tanks in Afghanistan are a form of line-of-sight, direct-fire artillery, like very big rifles, and when they are used, they are employed statically and individually. The ANA's 20 tanks are an unreliable parade force.[337]

On the other hand, the ARVN **did** have tanks, lots of them, and lots of experience in operating them in a combined arms role.[338] In 1970, the ARVN had four brigades of tanks,[339] largely M-48 Pattons, which were a proven tactical match for the NVA's T-55.[340] Each ARVN armor brigade headquarters was "highly mobile, track-mounted, packed with radio gear, and manned by a carefully selected, battle-tested staff."[341] The ARVN and the NVA had relative armor parity. Thus, the real comparison is not between the NVA and the Taliban in terms of opposing combat power and external support, it is between the Taliban and the ANA, and in terms of heavy weapons, both are roughly evenly matched. The Taliban vs. the ANA is and will be a light infantry vs. light infantry war (see Appendix II).

Top, the Taliban have experience operating tanks, and, increasingly, Humvees, bottom.

## Picture I-12. Taliban Tanks and Humvees.

Arguments about relative force size are also red herrings. To argue that the Taliban has only x number of fighters (and substitute for x with whatever intelligence estimate one prefers) is a profound miscomprehension of the various groups that loosely comprise the Taliban. While the number of men in the ANA basically represents the maximum number it can field, because the maximum annual number of recruits has balanced out with annual attrition, this is not true of the Taliban. The number of fighters in the field today merely represents the number current Taliban leadership believes to be appropriate for its current operational goals. In fact, there are hundreds of thousands of young men in northern Pakistan steeped in militant *jihad* in the radical madrassas which abound in the region, and who are ready and eager to martyr themselves in *jihad* in Afghanistan.[342] As long as American airpower remains a daily threat, massing such forces would result in mass casualties for little gain, as Taliban leadership is keenly aware. But whether the Taliban has 20,000 or 30,000 or 23,871 fighters in Afghanistan today is irrelevant; unlike the ANA, it is able to "surge" quickly and escalate violence rapidly, given logistic support from the Pakistani Army of the type provided from 1996 to 2001. The year 2013 witnessed Taliban forces massing in the hundreds for the first time,[343] with more such larger formations in 2014,[344] a classic indicator of a late-stage insurgency.[345]

In addition, the Taliban can rely to a great extent on the "snowball" and "hanger-on" effects of the Afghan Way of War,[346] seen so dramatically between 1996 and 2001, in which Taliban forces assimilated fighters from overrun local militias into their ranks like a snowball rolling down a hill. This is inevitable with ALP forces; the choice presented in the Afghan Way of War is always "join us or die."[347] Perversely, training and equipping the ALP ultimately may be tantamount to the Taliban outsourcing this function to the United States. From 1996 to 2001, the Taliban also absorbed previously uncommitted young men along the way to national power who suddenly saw benefits in the form of loot, plunder, rapine, food, and especially social prestige from "hanging-on" to the Taliban as it went by. This will certainly happen again in Pashtun areas. The ANA will have neither of these traditional Afghan force generators. Even combat losses today in Helmand are difficult to replace, and it was only the insertion of one of the ANA commando battalions into Helmand by air, rather than new replacements, combined with the massive application of U.S. CAS, that stabilized the situation in September and October 2014. Without U.S. airpower, the ANA garrison in the town of Sangin was overrun on November 29, 2014, killing 14 ANA soldiers and leaving another six or seven MIA.[348]

Furthermore, in the summer of 2014, the highly motivated but lightly armed ISIS in Iraq faced a numerically far superior and more heavily armed Iraqi Army, which was equipped with armor and artillery, and rolled over them in a matter of hours. Perhaps as good or better a comparison than NVA vs. ARVN for the future of Afghanistan is ISIS vs. the Iraqi Army.

For the Taliban, analyzing their campaign to regain power in Western terms of the tactical, operational, and strategic levels of war, tactical success might be said to take the form of temporarily overrunning police checkpoints and inflicting steady casualties on the police and army. This they are already achieving on a daily basis. Operational success for the Taliban, although they do not think about it in these terms, might be evaluated as briefly capturing a provincial capital, or taking and holding several contiguous district centers, to give themselves a base of uncontested local power. The Taliban extended the traditional fighting season into December in 2014 to achieve this in Helmand province. Dr. Abdul Hamidi, the chief of medical services for the ANP in Helmand told *The New York Times* in mid-December 2014 that "the Quetta Shura has a big push to raise their flags over three districts by January, and has ordered their people to keep fighting until they do."[349] Strategic success for the Taliban in the next 2 years might be described in Western terms as perhaps taking and holding an entire province and its provincial capital, from which they could proclaim the return of the "Islamic State of Afghanistan" to Afghan soil. This would be an enormous propaganda victory for the Taliban, and a major and demoralizing defeat for the Afghan government. This is unlikely in 2015, but in this sense, the Taliban only has to succeed in one province in 2015 and subsequent years, while the ANA and ANP have to succeed in all 34 provinces. The ANA and ANP must spread themselves out thinly and defend the government presence country-wide, while the Taliban can mass and choose the time and place of their attacks. In 2015, as in 2014, the military initiative will be entirely in the hands of the Taliban. In 2015, the Taliban would only need to win one big battle to achieve something akin to strategic success; the security forces need to win them all to prevent it.

## ENDNOTES—PART 1

1. Franck Salameh, *Language, Memory, and Identity in the Middle East: The Case for Lebanon*, Plymouth, UK: Lexington Books, 2010, p. 259.

2. "Why 'Magical Thinking' Works for Some People," *Scientific American*, October 19, 2010, available from *www.scientificamerican.com/article/superstitions-can-make-you/*.

3. "Afghanistan Gains Will Be Lost Quickly after Drawdown, U.S. Intelligence Estimate Warns," *The Washington Post*, December 28, 2013, available from *www.washingtonpost.com/world/national-security/afghanistan-gains-will-be-lost-quickly-after-drawdown-us-intelligence-estimate-warns/2013/12/28/ac609f90-6f32-11e3-aecc-85cb037b7236_story.html*.

4. "Petraeus Tells CIA to Consult Troops on War in Afghanistan," Fox News, October 11, 2011, available from *www.foxnews.com/world/2011/10/14/petraeus-tells-cia-to-consult-troops-on-war-in-*

*afghanistan/*; Michael O'Hanlon, "The Intelligence Assessment Is Too Pessimistic about Afghanistan," *The Washington Post*, January 3, 2014, available from *www.mobygroup.com/moby-media-up-date/mmu-archives-2014/1019-mmu-the-intelligence-assessment-is-too-pessimistic-about-afghanistan-03-january-2014.*

5. "US Intelligence Report Contradicts Pentagon's View Regarding Progress in Afghanistan," TACSTRAT, Tactical Knowledge for Strategic Development, January 17, 2012, available from *tacstrat.com/content/index.php/2012/01/17/us-intelligence-report-contradicts-pentagons-view-regarding-progress-in-afghanistan/.*

6. *Ibid.*

7. "The Effort To Begin Withdrawing US Military Personnel From Vietnam," Washington, DC: Central Intelligence Agency (CIA) Library, available from *https://www.cia.gov/library/center-for-the-study-of-intelligence/csi-publications/books-and-books/cia-and-the-vietnam-policymakers-three-episodes-1962-1968/epis1.html.*

8. Scott Plous, *The Psychology of Judgment and Decision Making*, New York: McGraw-Hill, 1993.

9. Chap. 4, "U.S. and France in Indochina, 1950-56," The Pentagon Papers, Gravel Ed., Vol. 1, Boston, MA: Beacon Press, 1971, Sec. 1, pp. 179-214.

10. Musa Khan Jalalzai, *Whose Army? Afghanistan's Future and the Blueprint for Civil War*, New York: Algora Publishing, 2014, p. 6.

11. Masato Toriya, "Afghanistan as a Buffer State between Regional Powers in the Late Nineteenth Century: An Analysis of Internal Politics Focusing on the Local Actors and the British Policy," Regional Powers, Cross-Disciplinary Studies, Sapporo, Japan: Slavic Research Center, Hokkaido University, available from *https://src-h.slav.hokudai.ac.jp/rp/publications/no14/14-05_Toriya.pdf.*

12. John Seeley, "We seem, as it were, to have conquered and peopled half the world in a fit of absence of mind," *The Expansion of England: Two Courses of Lectures*, London, UK: MacMillan & Co., 1883, p. 8.

13. Gertrude Bell, *Bahman Maghsoudlou, Grass: Untold Stories*, Costa Mesa, CA: Mazda Publishers, Inc., 2009, p. 176. Ruth Lapidoth, "Treaty of Mohammara," *The Red Sea and the Gulf of Aden*, Vol. 5, The Hague, The Netherlands: Martinus Nijhoff Publishers, 1982, p. 59.

14. Jeffrey Record, *The Wrong War: Why We Lost in Vietnam*, Monterey, CA: Naval Institute Press, 1998, Chap. 1.

15. Azam Ahmed, "Hours' Drive Outside Kabul, Taliban Reign," *The New York Times*, November 22, 2014.

16. The former location of Forward Operating Base Todd.

17. "Clash in Badghis Kills 6 ANA," *TOLOnews.com*, December 2, 2014.

18. "Taliban Overrun an Afghan Army Base," *The New York Times*, November 29, 2014.

19. "Guide to the Analysis of Insurgency," Washington, DC: CIA, released January 5, 2009, p. 11.

20. Walter Capps, ed., *The Vietnam Reader*, New York: Routledge, 1991, p. 106.

21. Historical Division of the Joint Secretariat, *The History of the Joint Chiefs of Staff: The Joint Chiefs of Staff and the War in Vietnam 1969-1970*, Washington, DC: Joint Chiefs of Staff, 1976, p. 207.

22. "South Vietnam — Civil Self-Defense Force / People's Self-Defense Force," *GlobalSecurity.org*, available from *www.globalsecurity.org/military/world/vietnam/rvn-self-defense-force.htm*.

23. *The History of the Joint Chiefs of Staff: The Joint Chiefs of Staff and the War in Vietnam 1969-1970*, p. 207.

24. R. W. Komer, "Impact of Pacification on Insurgency in South Vietnam," The Komer Report, Santa Monica, CA: The Rand Corporation, August 1970, available from *www.rand.org/content/dam/rand/pubs/papers/2008/P4443.pdf*.

25. RC South and RC Southwest are comprised of the following provinces: Zabul: 6,696 square miles, Kandahar: 20,858 square miles, Daykundi: 6,984 square miles, Uruzgan: 4,880 square miles, Helmand: 22,619 square miles, and Nimruz: 15,832 square miles.

26. Excludes Afghan diaspora resident in Pakistan and Iran. See *The World Factbook*, Washington, DC: CIA, 2010.

27. Ian S. Livingston and Michael O'Hanlon, "Afghanistan Index, Also Including Selected Data on Pakistan," Washington, DC: The Brookings Institute, January 10, 2014, available from *www. brookings.edu/~/media/Programs/foreign%20policy/afghanistan%20 index/index20140110.pdf.*

28. Fabrizio Foschini, "Changing of the Guards: Is the APPF Program Coming to an End?" The Afghan Analysts Network, March 8, 2014, available from *https://www.afghanistan-analysts.org/ changing-of-the-guards-is-the-appf-program-coming-to-an-end/.*

29. "Departing U.S. General Says Afghan Forces 'Inept' at Basic Motor Repairs," *Reuters*, Kabul, Afghanistan, December 11, 2104, available from *www.reuters.com/article/2014/12/11/us-afghan-istan-usa-idUSKBN0JP0H120141211.* On December 11, 2014, departing ISAF Commander Lieutenant General Joseph Anderson told *Reuters* news agency that 20 percent of the 195,000 ANA billets on paper are unfilled.

30. "Iraq: Population," *Countryeconomy.com*, available from *countryeconomy.com/demography/population/iraq.*

31. *Army Field Manual (FM) 3-24/Marine Corps Warfighting Publication (MCWP) 3-33.5, Insurgencies and Countering Insurgencies,* Washington, DC: DoD, December 15, 2006, pp. 1-13. Italics added.

32. Jeffrey A. Friedman, "Manpower and Counterinsurgency, Empirical Foundations for Theory and Doctrine," *Security Studies,* Vol. 20, No. 4, 2011, pp. 556-591.

33. Livingston and O'Hanlon, "Afghanistan Index, Also Including Selected Data on Pakistan."

34. James Willbanks, *The Battle of an Loc*, Bloomington, IN: The Indiana University Press, 2005, p. 2.

35. Author's recollection.

36. *Ibid.*

37. Approximately 15,000 men in 22 regular ARVN Ranger Battalions in 10 Groups, and 33 Border Ranger Battalions in five groups with a strength of 14,365 men.

38. Lieutenant General (Ret.) Burton Patrick, "ARVN Rangers," *Untold Stories*, available from *vnafmamn.com/ARVN_Rangers.html*.

39. "Afghanistan National Army: Commando Brigade," *Afghanistan Army*, available from *www.crwflags.com/fotw/flags/af%5Eana.html#comm*.

40. "In Afghanistan, Army Struggles to Wage War with Damaged Equipment, Poor Logistics," *The Washington Post*, October 13, 2013, available from *www.washingtonpost.com/world/asia_pacific/in-afghanistan-army-struggles-to-wage-war-with-damaged-equipment-poor-logistics/2013/10/17/96118b40-34e6-11e3-89db-8002ba99b894_story.html*.

41. Dan Nolan, "Amateurs Talk Tactics, Professionals Talk Logistics: Thinking About the Strategic Price of Oil," Washington, DC: Truman National Security Project, June 27, 2012, available from *trumanproject.org/doctrine-blog/amateurs-talk-tactics-professionals-talk-logistics-thinking-about-the-strategic-price-of-oil/*.

42. "Public Lecture and Open Discussion 'The Afghan National Army: Sustainability Challenges beyond Financial Aspects'," *ARU*, Tuesday, November 18, 2014, Kabul, Afghanistan: Afghanistan Research and Evaluation Unit, p. 5.

43. "Assessment of U.S. Government and Coalition Efforts to Develop the Logistics Sustainment Capability of the Afghan National Army," Report of the Inspector General, Report No. DODIG-2015-047, Washington, DC: DoD, December 19, 2014, available from *www.dodig.mil/pubs/documents/DODIG-2015-047.pdf*.

44. Interview with embedded U.S. advisor, October 12, 2014.

45. "Departing U.S. General Says Afghan Forces 'Inept' at Basic Motor Repairs."

46. See, for example, "Afghan Army Begins to Take the Lead," *The New York Times*, April 7, 2013, available from *www.nytimes. com/slideshow/2013/04/07/world/asia/20130408-AFGHANARMY. html#15*.

47. The main access road through Kunar Province, which runs parallel to the Durand Line, is nicknamed "Route California." David Kelly, *The Kunar ADT and the Afghan Coin Fight*, Bloomington, IN: Authorhouse, 2011, pp. 99, 106.

48. "At Afghan Military Hospital, Graft and Deadly Neglect," *The Wall Street Journal*, September 3, 2011, available from *online. wsj.com/articles/SB10001424053111904480904576496703389391710*.

49. "The Pentagon's Shocking Cover-Up of the Afghan National Military Hospital Scandal," Buzz Feed News, August 7, 2012, available from *www.buzzfeed.com/mhastings/exclusive-the-pentagons-shocking-cover-up-of-the*.

50. James Gibson, *The Perfect War: Technowar in Vietnam*, New York, Grove Press, December 1, 2007.

51. *Ibid.*

52. "Taliban Kill Seven Afghan Police Officers in Raid on Checkpoint," *The Guardian*, December 21, 2014, available from *www.theguardian.com/world/2014/dec/21/taliban-kill-afghan-police-checkpoint*.

53. "Public Lecture and Open Discussion 'The Afghan National Army: Sustainability Challenges beyond Financial Aspects'," *ARU*, Tuesday, November 18, 2014, p. 5.

54. Antonio Giustozzi, "The Afghan National Army: Sustainability Challenges Beyond Financial Aspects," Kabul, Afghanistan: Afghan Research and Evaluation Unit, February 2014, p. 8.

55. *Ibid.*

56. Fred Kaplan, "Who Disbanded the Iraqi Army?" *Slate*, September 7, 2007, available from *www.slate.com/articles/news_and_politics/war_stories/2007/09/who_disbanded_the_iraqi_army.html*.

57. "The Iraqi Army Never Was," *The American Conservative*, October 9, 2014, available from *www.theamericanconservative.com/articles/the-iraqi-army-never-was/*.

58. Michael O'Hanlon, "Why the World Shouldn't Write Off the Iraqi Army Just Yet," *Reuters*, October 22, 2014, available from *blogs.reuters.com/great-debate/2014/10/22/why-the-world-shouldnt-give-up-on-the-iraqi-army-just-yet/*.

59. "Iraq army Capitulates to Isis Militants in Four Cities," *The Guardian*, June 11, 2014, available from *www.theguardian.com/world/2014/jun/11/mosul-isis-gunmen-middle-east-states*.

60. Robert Mikesh, *Flying Dragons: The South Vietnamese Air Force*, Atglen, PA: Schiffer Publishing, 2005.

61. *The History of the Joint Chiefs of Staff: The Joint Chiefs of Staff and the War in Vietnam 1969-1970*, p. 197.

62. Author's professional recollection.

63. Interestingly, two of the ANAF helicopter pilots were women who flew many operational sorties. One was subsequently killed in an accident unrelated to her military duties.

64. "Afghan Air Force Ascent Slow, Imperiling Battle with Taliban," *Reuters*, January 25, 2015, available from *www.reuters.com/article/2015/01/26/us-afghanistan-airforce-idUSK-BN0KY10Z20150126*.

65. *Ibid.*

66. "Public Lecture and Open Discussion 'The Afghan National Army: Sustainability Challenges beyond Financial Apsects',"*ARU*, Tuesday, November 18, 2014, p. 7.

67. "Afghan Air Force (AAF)," *Afghan War News*, available from *www.afghanwarnews.info/air/afghanairforce.htm#Endnotes*.

68. "SNC, Embraer Deliver First A-29 to US Air Force," *Defense News*, September 25, 2014, available from *www.defensenews.com/article/20140925/DEFREG02/309250042/SNC-Embraer-Deliver-First-29-US-Air-Force*.

69. "MD Helicopters Awarded $44M More for Afghan MD530F Weapon System," Helihub, October 2, 2014, available from *helihub.com/2014/10/02/md-helicopters-awarded-44m-more-for-afghan-md530f-weapon-system/*.

70. "Delivery of 63 Mi-17V-5 Helicopters to Afghan Air Force Completed," Kabul, Afghanistan: Khaama Press, October 31, 2014, available from *www.khaama.com/delivery-of-63-mi-17v-5-helicopters-to-afghan-air-force-completed-8691*.

71. "Afghan Air Force Ascent Slow, Imperiling Battle with Taliban."

72. "Afghan Air Force Probed in Drug Running," *The Wall Street Journal*, March 10, 2012; "Afghan Air Force Suspected of Drug Running: Report," ABC News, March 8, 2012; "Afghan Air Force: Flying Drug Mules That Fuel Civil War," Danger Room at *Wired.com*, March 8, 2012.

73. "Ties to Russia Arms Supplier Snarl U.S. Sanctions Efforts," *The Wall Street Journal*, March 26, 2014, available from *www.wsj.com/articles/SB10001424052702304688104579467542674720908*.

74. "SIGAR Audit 13-13: Afghan Special Mission Wing: DOD Moving Forward with $771.8 Million Purchase of Aircraft that the Afghans Cannot Operate and Maintain," Washington, DC: SIGAR, p. 7, available from *www.sigar.mil/pdf/audits/2013-05-27-audit-13-13.pdf*.

75. *Ibid.*

76. Michael C. Veneri, "Multiplying by Zero," *Military Review*, January-February 2011, available from *www.au.af.mil/au/awc/awcgate/milreview/veneri_janfeb2011.pdf*.

77. *Ibid.*, pp. 89-90.

78. "Islamist Militancy in the Pakistan-Afghanistan Border Region and U.S. Policy," Washington, DC: Congressional Research Service, November 21, 2008, p. CRS-8, fn 21.

79. Frank Clements, *Conflict in Afghanistan: a Historical Encyclopedia*, Santa Barbara, CA: ABC-CLIO, 2003, p. 54. "Afghanistan: Arena for a New Rivalry," *The Washington Post*, September 16, 1998, available from *pqasb.pqarchiver.com/washingtonpost/doc/408407755. html?FMT=ABS&FMTS=ABS:FT&type=current&date=Sep%20 16,%201998&author=Pamela%20Constable&pub=The%20Washington%20Post&edition=&startpage=&desc=Afghanistan:%20 Arena%20for%20a%20New%20Rivalry*; Consular Officer Brad Hansen, U.S. Consulate (Peshawar) Cable, "Afghanistan: A Report of Pakistani Military Assistance to the Taliban," March 24, 1998, Declassified. The Taliban File, Part I, Document 26, Washington, DC: The National Security Archive, The George Washington University, available from *www2.gwu.edu/~nsarchiv/NSAEBB/ NSAEBB97/tal25.pdf*.

80. Roger Boniface, *MIGs over North Vietnam: The Vietnam People's Air Force in Combat, 1965-75*, Mechanicsburg, PA: Stackpole Military History, 2010.

81. "The Modern Iraqi Military is on a Path of Slow Recovery after the U.S. Invasion of 2013," *Global Fire Power*, March 27, 2014, available from *www.globalfirepower.com/country-military-strength-detail.asp?country_id=iraq*.

82. *Ibid.*

83. "Iraq's Air Force," *The Huffington Post*, August 23, 2014, available from *www.huffingtonpost.com/chris-weigant/iraqs-air-force_b_5523840.html*.

84. "Iraq Cobbling Together Makeshift Air Force to Fight ISIS," *The Washington Post*, June 27, 2014, available from *www. washingtonpost.com/world/2014/06/27/be172f43-cf98-4677-8e6d-4d64a5ae5e1d_story.html*.

85. *The Aviationist*, available from *theaviationist.com/tag/iraqi-air-force/*.

86. Valéry Tarrius, "La Police de Campagne du Sud-Vietnam 1967-1975" ("The Police of the South Vietnam Campaign 1967-1975"), Paris, France: Armes Militaria Magazine, Histoire & Collections, March 2005, pp. 37–43.

87. Thi Minh-Phuong Ngo, *Education and Agricultural Growth in Vietnam*, Madison, WI: Department of Agricultural and Applied Economics, University of Wisconsin-Madison, 2006, p. 14, available from *perso.fundp.ac.be/~tpngo/Education_WPjun06.pdf*.

88. "Illiteracy Slows Afghan Army, U.S. Pullout, " CBS News September 14, 2009, available from *www.cbsnews.com/news/illiteracy-slows-afghan-army-us-pullout/*.

89. Kenneth Katzman, "Afghanistan: Post-Taliban Governance, Security, and U.S. Policy," Washington, DC: Congressional Research Service, December 2, 2014, p. 32, available from *www.fas.org/sgp/crs/row/RL30588.pdf*.

90. Antonio Giustozzi and Mohammed Isaqzadeh, *Policing Afghanistan: The Politics of the Lame Leviathan*, Oxford, UK: Oxford University Press, 2013, p. 74.

91. *Ibid.*

92. "Police Transition in Afghanistan," Washington, PA: U.S. Institute of Peace, February 2013, p. 5, available from *www.usip.org/sites/default/files/SR322.pdf*.

93. "Afghan National Police:.More than $300 Million in Annual, U.S.-funded Salary Payments Is Based on Partially Verified or Reconciled Data," SIGAR 15-26 Audit Report, Washington, DC: SIGAR, January 2015, available from *www.sigar.mil/pdf/audits/SIGAR-15-26-AR.pdf*.

94. *Ibid.*, p. 6.

95. *Ibid.*

96. "Watchdog: US May Be Paying Salaries of 'Ghost' Afghan Policemen," *Stars and Stripes*, March 19, 2014, available from *www.stripes.com/news/watchdog-us-may-be-paying-salaries-of-ghost-afghan-policemen-1.273607*.

97. "Afghan National Police: More than $300 Million in Annual, U.S.-funded Salary Payments Is Based on Partially Verified or Reconciled Data," p. 5.

98. *Ibid.*, p. 6.

99. *Ibid.*, p. 7.

100. "Afghan Forces Stagger through First Test," *Asia Times*, November 5, 2013, available from *www.atimes.com/atimes/South_Asia/SOU-01-051113.html*.

101. "Afghan Forces' Casualties 'Not Sustainable,' U.S. Commander Says," *The Washington Post*, November 5, 2014, available from *www.washingtonpost.com/world/national-security/afghan-forces-casualties-not-sustainable-us-commander-says/2014/11/05/a3df595a-6514-11e4-bb14-4cfea1e742d5_story.html*.

102. "Major Incidents of Terrorist Violence in Jammu and Kashmir 2014," *South Asia Terrorism Portal*, available from *www.satp.org/satporgtp/countries/india/states/jandk/data_sheets/majorincidents2014.htm*.

103. "Guide to the Analysis of Insurgency," p. 11.

104. *Ibid.*

105. "Afghanistan Police Corruption Is Fuelling Insurgency," *The Telegraph*, June 3, 2010, available from *www.telegraph.co.uk/news/worldnews/asia/afghanistan/7801459/Afghanistan-police-corruption-is-fuelling-insurgency.html*.

106. "Afghanistan in 2013, A Survey of the Afghan People," Washington, DC: The Asia Foundation, 2013, available from *asiafoundation.org/resources/pdfs/2013AfghanSurvey.pdf*.

107. *Ibid.*

108. "Afghanistan Police Corruption Is Fuelling Insurgency."

109. "This is What Winning Looks Like," YouTube, Vice News, posted May 27, 2013, available from *https://www.youtube.com/watch?v=Ja5Q75hf6QI*.

110. "Afghan Forces' Casualties 'Not Sustainable,' U.S. Commander Says."

111. "Afghan Official: Insurgents Kill 9 Police," *The Sun Herald*, January 4, 2015.

112. *Ibid.*

113. "Police Officer Killed in Afghanistan Blast," Z News, January 12, 2015, available from *zeenews.india.com/news/india/police-officer-killed-in-afghanistan-blast_1528916.html*.

114. "Afghan forces' Casualties 'not Sustainable,' U.S. Commander Says."

115. *Ibid.*

116. *Ibid.*

117. Azam Ahmed.

118. "Truth, Lies and Afghanistan," *The Armed Forces Journal*, February 1, 2012, available from *www.armedforcesjournal.com/truth-lies-and-afghanistan/*.

119. *Ibid.*

120. Jim Randle, "Study Finds Iraqi National Police Ineffective in Combating Terrorism," Voice of America (VOA) News, October 14, 2007.

121. "Iraq, Education in Transition Needs and Challenges 2004," Paris, France: United Nations Educational, Scientific and Cultural Organization (UNESCO), 2004, available from *www.unesco.org/education/iraq/na_13jan2005.pdf*.

122. William Rosenau, *US Internal Security Assistance to South Vietnam: Insurgency, Subversion and Public Order*, New York: Routledge, 2007, p. 128.

123. "Taliban Push into Afghan Districts that U.S. Had Secured," *The New York Times*, December 22, 2014, available from *www.nytimes.com/2014/12/23/world/taliban-push-into-afghan-districts-that-us-had-secured.html?_r=0*.

124. "Insurgents in Afghanistan's Laghman Province May Win by not Losing," *Stars and Stripes*, November 14, 2014, available from *www.stripes.com/news/middle-east/insurgents-in-afghanistan-s-laghman-province-may-win-by-not-losing-1.314358*.

125. "An Army for Afghanistan," *The New York Times*, December 15, 2014.

126. "Misgivings by U.S. General as Afghanistan Mission Ends," *The New York Times*, December 8, 2014, available from *www.nytimes.com/2014/12/09/world/asia/us-general-joseph-anderson-mission-in- afghanistan.html?_r=1*.

127. "No Coordination between Security Agencies: Ghani," *TOLOnews.com*, December 15, 2014.

128. "Departing U.S. General Says Afghan Forces 'Inept' at Basic Motor Repairs."

129. "Afghan Police Lead Insurgent Fight at High Cost," Associated Press, December 28, 2014, available from *abcnews.go.com/International/wireStory/afghan-police-lead-insurgent-fight-high-cost-27859001*.

130. Azam Ahmed.

131. *Ibid.*

132. *Ibid.*

133. *Ibid.*

134. The Combined Action Platoon (CAP) program was well described by former Marine and DoD official Bing West in *The Village*, New York: Harper and Row, 1972.

135. "Afghanistan: Annual Report on Protection of Civilians in Armed Conflict," Kabul, Afghanistan: United Nations Assistance Mission in Afghanistan (UNAMA), March 2011, p. 33.

136. West.

137. "Village Stability Operations (VSO)," *Afghan War News*, available from *www.afghanwarnews.info/security/village-stability-operations-vso.htm*.

138. Lewis Walt, *Strange War, Strange Strategy: A General's Report on the War in Vietnam*, New York: Funk and Wagnalls, 1970, p. 105.

139. Max Boot, "The Lessons of a Quagmire," *The New York Times*, November 26, 2003.

140. "Independent Assessment of the Afghan National Security Forces," Appendix E, Table 42, Arlington, VA: Center for Naval Analysis, January 2014, pp. 319-324, available from *www.cna.org/sites/default/files/research/CNA%20Independent%20Assessment%20of%20the%20ANSF.pdf*.

141. Robert Hulslander and Jake Spivey, "Village Stability Operations and Afghan Local Police," *Prism 3*, No. 3, 2012, p. 132.

142. "Afghanistan: Annual Report on Protection of Civilians in Armed Conflict," p. 33.

143. Graham Cosmas and Terrence Murray, *U.S. Marines in Vietnam: Vietnamization and Redeployment, 1970–1971*, History and Museums Division, Headquarters, U.S. Marine Corps, Washington, DC: Superintendent of Documents, U.S. Government Printing Office (USGPO), 1986, p. 139.

144. James Gibson, *The Perfect War: Technowar in Vietnam*, New York: Grove Press, December 1, 2007.

145. "Afghanistan: Annual Report on Protection of Civilians in Armed Conflict, p. 33.

146. Mark Brown, Jr., "Village Stability Operations: An Historical Perspective from Vietnam to Afghanistan," *The Long War Journal*, March 28, 2013, available from *smallwarsjournal.com/jrnl/art/village-stability-operations-an-historical-perspective-from-vietnam-to-afghanistan*.

147. *Ibid.*

148. "No Time to Lose: Promoting the Accountability of the Afghan National Security Forces," *Oxfam*, No. 10, May 2011, p. 8.

149. "Afghanistan: Annual Report on Protection of Civilians in Armed Conflict," p. 31.

150. "Document - Getting away with Murder? The Impunity of International Forces in Afghanistan," *Amnesty International*, February 26, 2009, available from *https://www.amnesty.org/en/documents/ASA11/001/2009/en/*. See also "Afghanistan—Kandahar Death Squads," Channel 14 News, available from *www.journeyman.tv/?lid=60529&tmpl=transcript*; and "U.S. Covert Paramilitary Presence in Afghanistan much Larger than Thought," *The Washington Post*, September 22, 2010, available from *www.washingtonpost.com/wp-dyn/content/article/2010/09/22/AR2010092206241.html*.

151. "U.S. Covert Paramilitary Presence in Afghanistan much Larger than Thought."

152. "Exclusive: CIA Falls Back in Afghanistan," The Daily Beast, April 5, 2014, available from *www.thedailybeast.com/articles/2014/05/04/exclusive-cia-falls-back-in-afghanistan.html#*.

153. "CIA Trains Covert Units of Afghans to Continue the Fight against Taliban," *The Independent*, July 20, 2011, available from *www.independent.co.uk/news/world/asia/cia-trains-covert-units-of-afghans-to-continue-the-fight-against-taliban-2317182.html*.

154. *Ibid.*

155. "A US-Backed Militia Runs Amok in Afghanistan," *Al Jazeera*, July 23, 2014, available from *america.aljazeera.com/articles/2014/7/23/exclusive-a-killinginandar.html*.

156. "After America," *The New Yorker*, June 9, 2012, available from *www.newyorker.com/magazine/2012/07/09/after-america-2.*

157. Katzman.

158. "No Time to Lose," p. 8.

159. "US-Trained Afghan Police Guilty of Abuse, Report Finds," British Broadcasting Corporation, December 16, 2011, available from *www.bbc.co.uk/news/world-asia-16211543*.

160. "No Time to Lose,"p. 8.

161. "As U.S. Scales Back in Afghanistan, Local Defense Program Expands," *San Diego Union Tribune*, August 15, 2011, available from *www.utsandiego.com/news/2011/aug/15/us-scales-back-afghanistan-local-defense-program-e/2/?#article-copy*.

162. "Afghanistan: Annual Report on Protection of Civilians in Armed Conflict," pp. 32-33.

163. "Afghan Local Police Group Deserts to Taliban-Led Insurgents," *The Washington Post*, July 4, 2012, available from *www.washingtonpost.com/world/war-zones/afghan-local-police-group-deserts-to- taliban-led-insurgents/2012/07/04/gJQAzvNCNW_story.html*.

164. "6 Afghan Local Police Officer [sic] Surrender to Taliban in Ghor," Kabul, Afghanistan: Khaama Press, June 17, 2013, available from *www.khaama.com/afghan-local-police-officer-surrender-to-taliban-in-ghor-2195*.

165. Hulslander and Spivey, p. 127.

166. "Taliban Return to Afghan Town that Rose Up and Drove Out Its Leaders," *The Guardian*, October 27, 2014, available from *www.theguardian.com/world/2014/oct/27/taliban-return-afghan-town-gizab*.

167. "Local Police Selling Weapons and Ammunition to Taliban," Kabul, Afghanistan: Khaama Press, November 3, 2014.

168. "Insurgents in Afghanistan's Laghman Province May Win by not Losing."

169. Seth Jones, "Afghanistan Redux: Countering the Taliban Insurgency," V. Krishnappa, Shanthis D'Souza, Priyanka Singh, eds., *Saving Afghanistan*, New Delhi, India: Academic Foundation, 2009, p. 69.

170. "Insurgents in Afghanistan's Laghman Province May Win by not Losing."

171. *Ibid.*

172. See, for example, "Bring Back the Bad Guys," *The American Conservative*, January 1, 2010, available from *www.theamericanconservative.com/articles/bring-back-the-bad-guys/*.

173. Boot.

174. "Bomb Explodes at Funeral in Pakistan," National Public Radio, September 15, 2011, available from *www.npr.org/2011/09/15/140508406/bomb-explodes-at-funeral-in-pakistan*.

175. Report of the UNHCR Sub-Office Jalalabad of 8/10/2002, Geneva, Switzerland: Office of the United Nations High Commissioner for Refugees, available from *www.aims.org.af/afg/dist_profiles/unhcr_district_profiles/eastern/kunar/dangam.pdf*.

176. "Pakistani Taliban Squeezed by Afghan Revolt, U.S. Drone Strikes," *Reuters*, December 4, 2014, available from *www.reuters.com/article/2014/12/04/us-pakistan-afghanistan-taliban-idUSKCN0JI0XD20141204*.

177. "Bomb Explodes at Funeral In Pakistan."

178. "Kurds Advance against IS Group in Syria's Kobani." *The Daily Mail*, December 20, 2014, available from *www.dailymail.co.uk/wires/ap/article-2881727/Kurds-advance-against-IS-group-Syrias-Kobani.html*.

179. Thomas Johnson and Chris Mason, "No Sign until the Burst of Fire: Understanding the Pakistan-Afghanistan Frontier," *International Security*, Vol. 32, Issue 4, Spring 2008, Harvard University: The Belfer Center, pp. 41-77.

180. Giustozzi, "The Afghan National Army: Sustainability Challenges Beyond Financial Aspects," pp. 21-22.

181. "Investigation: Friendly Fire Airstrike that Killed U.S. Special Forces Was Avoidable," *The Washington Post*, September 4, 2014, available from *www.washingtonpost.com/news/checkpoint/wp/2014/09/04/investigation-friendly-fire-airstrike-that-killed-u-s-special-forces-was-avoidable/*.

182. Giustozzi, "The Afghan National Army: Sustainability Challenges Beyond Financial Aspects," p. 22.

183. Public discussion with senior analyst, October 12, 2014.

184. "U.S. Airstrikes Remain Crucial to Afghan Forces in Taliban Battles," *The Los Angeles Times*, December 28, 2014, available from *www.latimes.com/world/afghanistan-pakistan/la-fg-afghanistan-us-military-20141228-story.html#page=1*.

185. *Joint Publication (JP) 3-09.3, Joint Air Support*, Washington, DC: Joint Chiefs of Staff, available from *www.fas.org/irp/doddir/dod/jp3_09_3.pdf*.

186. Giustozzi, "The Afghan National Army: Sustainability Challenges Beyond Financial Aspects," p. 8.

187. "Smaller NATO Mission Has Big Job to Train Afghan Army in Time," *Reuters*, January 6, 2015.

188. Correspondence with the author, January 2, 2015.

189. "In a Shift, Obama Extends U.S. Role in Afghan Combat," *The New York Times*, November 21, 2014, available from *www.nytimes.com/2014/11/22/us/politics/in-secret-obama-extends-us-role-in-afghan-combat.html*.

190. "Obama Announces Afghanistan Troop Withdrawal Plan," CNN, June 23, 2011, available from *www.cnn.com/2011/POLITICS/06/22/afghanistan.troops.drawdown/*.

191. Johnson and Mason, "No Sign until the Burst of Fire."

192. "Taliban Attacks on 'Death Road' Highlight Continuing Persecution of Afghanistan's Hazaras," Associated Press, January 22, 2014, available from *www.foxnews.com/world/2014/01/22/taliban-attacks-on-death-road-highlight-continuing-persecution-afghanistan/*.

193 . "Will Hazaras Be Safe in Afghanistan after NATO's Pull-out?" Hazara People International Network, July 28, 2014, available from *www.hazarapeople.com/2014/07/28/will-hazaras-be-safe-in-afghanistan-after-natos-pullout/*.

194. Report of the Office of the Special Inspector General for Afghanistan Reconstruction (SIGAR), 1st Quarter 2014, April 30, 2014, p. iv, available from *www.sigar.mil/pdf/quarterlyreports/2014-04-30qr.pdf*. "SIGAR's auditors found that the single biggest issue limiting collection of customs revenues is corruption. Moreover, U.S. advisors report that Afghan employees who try to properly collect customs duties have been kidnapped and intimidated."

195. "How the U.S. Killed the Wrong Afghans," *Time Magazine*, February 6, 2002, available from *content.time.com/time/world/article/0,8599,198864,00.html*.

196. Brian Williams, *Afghanistan Declassified: A Guide to America's Longest War*, Philadelphia, PA: University of Pennsylvania Press, 2012, p. 62.

197. "System Failure: Anthropologists on the Battlefield," *USA Today*, August 11, 2013, available from *www.usatoday.com/story/nation/2013/08/11/human-terrain-system-afghanistan-war-anthropologists/2640297/*.

198. Shaista Wahab and Barry Youngerman, *A Brief History of Afghanistan*, New York: InfoBase Publishing, 2007, p. 13.

199. Anthony Arnold, *Afghanistan's Two-Party Communism: Parcham and Khalq*, Stanford, CA: Hoover Press, 1984.

200. Barnett R. Rubin, *The Fragmentation of Afghanistan*, New Haven, CT: Yale University Press, 2002, p. 105.

201. "The Soviet Occupation of Afghanistan," PBS Newshour, October 10, 2006, available from *www.pbs.org/newshour/updates/asia-july-dec06-soviet_10-10/*.

202. Steve Coll, *Ghost Wars*, New York: Penguin Books, 2004.

203. *Ibid.*

204. The Hazaras were represented by the "Tehran Eight," a group of eight Shi's mujahideen groups composed of (1) the Afghan Hezbollah, led by Karim Agmadi Yak Daste, (2) the Nasr Party, led by Muhammad Hussein Sadiqi, Abdul Ali Mazari and Shaykh Shafak, (3) the Corps of Islamic Revolution Guardians of Afghanistan, led by Sheikh Akbari, Mokhsem Rezai, and Sapake Pasdar, (4) the Islamic Movement of Afghanistan, led by Muhammad Asif Muhsini and Shaykh Sadeq Hashemi, (5) the Islamic Revolution Movement, led by Nasrullah Mansur, (6) Committee of Islamic Agreement (aka the "Shura Party"), led by Sayeed Ali Beheshti and Sayeed Djagran, (7) the Union of Islamic Fighters, led by Mosbah Sade, an Afghan Hazara leader from Bamian, and (8) the Raad ("Thunder") party, led by Shaykh Sayeed Abdul Jaffar Nadiri, and Muhammad Hazai Sayeed Ismail Balkhee. The Hizb-e Wahdat-e Islami Afghanistan was formed in Teheran as a united front to represent the Teheran Eight. The Hazaras were the second largest group of mujahideen after the Pashtuns. Thomas Ruttig, *Islamists, Leftists – and a Void in the Center. Afghanistan's Political Parties and where they come from (1902-2006)*, Kabul, Afghanistan: Konrad-Adenauer-Stiftung, Afghanistan Office, 2006.

205. Coll, Fn. 27.

206. These actions are generally interpreted by historians as the result of giving authority to local Soviet commanders to pacify their areas, rather than a deliberate policy of extermination orchestrated by army-level policy, not that it makes a great deal of difference in the long run.

207. Marek Sliwinski, "Afghanistan: The Decimation of a People," *Orbis*, Winter, 1989, p. 39.

208. "Remembering the 'Lion of Panjshir'," *Al Jazeera*, September 9, 2012, available from *www.aljazeera.com/indepth/features/2012/09/20129913233327927.html*.

209. Masood was assassinated by an al-Qaeda suicide team posing as Arab journalists 2 days before the attacks of September 11, 2001.

210. *Afghanistan: A Country Study*, Washington, DC: American University Press, 1986, pp. 288-289.

211. Giustozzi, "The Afghan National Army: Sustainability Challenges Beyond Financial Aspects," p. 10.

212. Forrest Marion, "The Destruction and Rebuilding of the Afghan Air Force, 1989-2009," *Air Power History*, June 2010, Joint Base Andrews, MD, Air Force Historical Foundation, available from *www.highbeam.com/doc/1G1-232177523.html*.

213. Clements, p. 54.

214. Seymour Hersh, *Chain of Command*, New York: Harper Collins, 2005, p. 132.

215. Ahmed Rashid, *Descent into Chaos: The United States and the Failure of Nation Building in Pakistan, Afghanistan, and Central Asia*, New York: Viking Press, 2008.

216. BBC News (October 26, 2011); Ahmed Rashid, "Secret Pakistan: Double Cross," *Descent into Chaos*.

217. "The ISI's Great Game in Afghanistan," *The Diplomat*, June 8, 2014; "Mistrust between Afghanistan and Pakistan soars as U.S. forces depart," *The Washington Post*, September 25, 2014.

218. "Pakistan's Spy Agency Is Tied to Attack on U.S. Embassy," *The New York Times*, September 22, 2011, available from *www.nytimes.com/2011/09/23/world/asia/mullen-asserts-pakistani-role-in-attack-on-us-embassy.html?pagewanted=all&_r=0*.

219. Thomas Johnson, "Financing Afghan Terrorism: Drugs, Thugs, and Creative Movements of Money," Jeanne K. Giraldo

and Harold A. Trinkunas, eds., *Terrorism Financing and State Responses: A Comparative Perspective*, Stanford, CA: Stanford University Press, 2007, p. 112.

220. "Can Iraq's Fate Befall Afghanistan?" *Al Jazeera*, June 21, 2014, available from *america.aljazeera.com/articles/2014/6/22/afghanistan-can-iraqscrisishappenheretoo.html*.

221. In late-2002, the author presented an unclassified State Department briefing to the interagency on the incipient insurgency in Afghanistan, using the CIA's unclassified "Guide to the Evaluation of Insurgencies" publication to cross walk events and developments on the ground in Afghanistan. The unclassified findings were pronounced "premature."

222. Spencer Ackerman, "How the CIA's Bags of Cash Undermined the Afghanistan War," *Wired.com*, April 29, 2013, available from *www.wired.com/2013/04/karzai-cia-money/*.

223. "Fraud and Folly in Afghanistan," *Foreign Policy*, September 23, 2014, available from *southasia.foreignpolicy.com/posts/2014/09/23/fraud_and_folly_in_afghanistan*.

224. "Afghan Army Death Rate Spikes 30 Percent," *Yahoo News*, October 3, 2014, available from *news.yahoo.com/afghan-army-death-rate-spikes-30-percent-071633638.html*.

225. "Fraud and Folly in Afghanistan," *Foreign Policy*, September 23, 2014, available from *southasia.foreignpolicy.com/posts/2014/09/23/fraud_and_folly_in_afghanistan*.

226. *Ibid.*

227. *Ibid.*

228. "Afghanistan in 2013: A Survey of the Afghan People."

229. Lodin was nominated by President Ghani for the post of Minister of Defense but Lodin withdrew his nomination after 48 hours.

230. Mohammadullah Halim Sirat, "Why Choose Ghani over Abdullah," *Pajhwok Afghan News*, June 11, p. 204, available

from *www.elections.pajhwok.com/en/content/why-choose-ghani-over-abdullah.*

231. Ahmed Rashid, "The Way Out of Afghanistan," *The New York Review of Books*, January 13, 2011, available from *www.nybooks.com/articles/archives/2011/jan/13/way-out-afghanistan/.*

232. "Afghan Projects, Officials in Limbo with Delay of Cabinet," *Daily Times*, December 3, 2014, available from *www.dailytimes.com.pk/region/03-Dec-2014/afghan-projects-officials-in-limbo-with-delay-of-cabinet.*

233. *Ibid.*

234. "Parliament Approves 9 of 19 Cabinet Nominees," *Tolo News*, January 28, 2015, available from *www.tolonews.com/en/afghanistan/17996-parliament-votes-on-cabinet-nominees.*

235. "The Warlord Who Defines Afghanistan: An Excerpt From Bruce Riedel's 'What We Won'," Washington, DC: The Brookings Institution, July 27, 2014, available from *www.brookings.edu/research/opinions/2014/07/27-warlord-who-defines-afghanistan-riedel.*

236. "Dostum Says 20,000 Special Force Set to Root Out Taliban," Kabul, Afghanistan: Khaama Press, January 1, 2015, available from *www.khaama.com/dostum-20-000-special-force-set-to-eliminate-taliban-2649/.*

237. Author's recollection.

238. "Quarterly Report to the United States Congress," Table 3.9, Washington, DC: SIGAR, April 30, 2014, p. 97.

239. Discussion with U.S. official in public forum, November 23, 2014.

240. "NATO Alarm over Afghan Army Crisis: Loss of Recruits Threatens Security as Handover Looms," *The Independent*, March 31, 2013, available from *www.independent.co.uk/news/world/asia/nato-alarm-over-afghan-army-crisis-loss-of-recruits-threatens-security-as-handover-looms-8555238.html.*

241. "Quarterly Report to the United States Congress," Table 3.9, p. 97.

242. "The Afghan National Security Forces Beyond 2014: Will They Be Ready?" eSeminar Series Primer Paper No. 2, Kitchener, Ontario, Canada: Center for Security Governance, February 2014, available from *www.ssrresourcecentre.org/wp-content/uploads/2014/02/eSeminar-Primer-No.-2.pdf*.

243. "A Force in Fragments: Reconstituting the Afghan National Army," Brussels, Belgium: International Crisis Group (ICG), Asia Report No. 190, May 12, 2010, p. 17, available from *www.crisisgroup.org/en/regions/asia/south-asia/afghanistan/190-a-force-in-fragments-reconstituting-the-afghan-national-army.aspx*.

244. Ira A. Hunt, Jr., *Losing Vietnam: How America Abandoned Southeast Asia*, Louisville, KY: University Press of Kentucky, 2013, pp. 111-112, 183.

245. Giustozzi, "The Afghan National Army: Sustainability Challenges Beyond Financial Aspects,"p. 10.

246. "NATO Alarm over Afghan Army Crisis: Loss of Recruits Threatens Security as Handover Looms."

247. Departing U.S. General Says Afghan Forces 'Inept' at Basic Motor Repairs."

248. "Afghanistan: 2014 and Beyond," Vienna, Austria: Austrian Federal Ministry of the Interior, 2014, p. 37, available from *www.bfa.gv.at/files/broschueren/AFGH_Bookie_2014_03.pdf*.

249. "Government of the Islamic Republic of Afghanistan Needs to Provide Better Accountability and Transparency Over Direct Contributions," Report of the Inspector General, Department of Defense Report No. DODIG-2014-102, Washington, DC: DoD, August 29, 2014, p. 17, available from *www.dodig.mil/pubs/documents/DODIG-2014-102.pdf*.

250. SIGAR Report to Congress, Washington, DC: U.S. Congress, January 30, 2013, pp. 73-74, cited in Anthony Cordesman, *The Afghan War in 2013: Meeting the Challenges of Transition*, Vol. III, draft, March 28, 2013, p. 58.

251. "Iraq Says It Found 50,000 "Ghost Soldiers" on Payroll," *Reuters*, December 1, 2014, available from *in.reuters.com/article/2014/12/01/mideast-crisis-iraq-soldiers-idINKCN0JF2RX20141201*.

252. "Public Lecture and Open Discussion 'The Afghan National Army: Sustainability Challenges beyond Financial Aspects'," *ARU*, Tuesday, November 18, 2014, p. 6.

253. "Departing U.S. General Says Afghan Forces 'Inept' at Basic Motor Repairs."

254. "Quarterly Report to the United States Congress," SIGAR, Table 3.9, p. 97.

255. *Ibid.*

256. *Ibid.*

257. 119,485 x .63 = 75,258.

258. Gary Owen, "Paint It Pink: The US Redefining ANA Success," *Afghan Analysts Network*, August 1, 2012, available from *www.afghanistan-analysts.org/paint-it-pink-the-us-redefining-ana-success/*; Gary Owen, "SIGAR: Widely Cited 352,000 ANSF Force Size Is Not Validated," *Empty Wheel*, March 27, 2013, available from *https://www.emptywheel.net/2013/03/27/sigar-widely-cited-352000-ansf-force-size-is-not-validated/*.

259. "Between April 2010 and August 2011, the International Joint Commission changed the Commander's Unit Assessment Tool rating definition level titles four times." See "Afghan National Security Forces: Actions Needed to Improve Plans for Sustaining Capability Assessment Efforts," SIGAR 14-33 Audit Report, SIGAR, February 5, 2014, available from *www.sigar.mil/pdf/audits/SIGAR_14-33-AR.pdf*.

260. "Taliban Attack Highly Regarded Afghan Army Unit," *The New York Times*, April 12, 2013, available from *www.nytimes.com/2013/04/13/world/asia/taliban-attacks-afghan-army-unit.html?pagewanted=all*.

261. *Ibid.*

262. "NATO Suddenly Classifies Ratings of Afghan Military and Police Capabilities," Washington, DC: Center for Public Integrity, October 30, 2014, available from *www.publicintegrity.org/2014/10/30/16130/nato-suddenly-classifies-ratings-afghan-military-and-police-capabilities.*

263. The decision to classify was not made at the request of the Afghan government, which considers the information to be unclassified, according to Khaama Press, available from *www.khaama.com/us-military-to-keep-secret-the-details-of-aid-to-afghan-forces-9910.* Other news organizations, including *Stars and Stripes, Al Jazeera, The Daily Caller,* and *Empty Wheel* reached the same conclusion. *The Daily Caller* referred to the decision as a "political move" ("Pentagon Spending In Afghanistan Just Got Way Less Transparent," *The Daily Caller,* January 29, 2015, available from *dailycaller.com/2015/01/29/pentagon-spending-in-afghanistan-just-got-way-less-transparent/*). The author's sources at the ICG in Kabul confirmed the decision to classify the information was unilateral.

264. "True State of Afghan Military Kept Secret, Report Says," NBC News, October 30, 2014, available from *www.nbcnews.com/news/investigations/true-state-afghan-military-kept-secret-report-says-n234866.*

265. Giustozzi, "The Afghan National Army: Sustainability Challenges Beyond Financial Aspects," graph 3, p. 10.

266. Interview with senior Afghan National Army officer, December 7, 2014.

267. FM 1-02, *Operational Terms and Graphics,* Appendix D, September 21, 2004, available from *https://rdl.train.army.mil/catalog-ws/view/100.ATSC/6C01FFE5-0DF6-415F-A13C-92ED36 A708CA-1303039189337/1-02/appd.htm.*

268. Giustozzi, "The Afghan National Army: Sustainability Challenges Beyond Financial Aspects," Table 1, p. 10. Afghan Army force size numbers for the years 1979-89 are derived from these sources: Nabi Misdaq, *Afghanistan: Political Frailty and External Interference,* Abingdon, Oxon, UK: Taylor & Francis, 2006;

David Isby, *Russia's War in Afghanistan*, Oxford, UK: Osprey Publishing, 1986, p. 18; Arnold, *Afghanistan's Two-party Communism*, p. 111; Phillip Bonosky, *Afghanistan–Washington's Secret War*, New York: International Publishers, 2001, p. 261; Bruce Amtstutz, *Afghanistan: The First Five Years of Soviet Occupation*, Washington, DC: National Defense University Press, 1986, pp. 180-181; Roger Kanet, *The Soviet Union, Eastern Europe, and the Third World*, Cambridge, UK: Cambridge University Press, 1987, p. 51; Roger Reese, *The Soviet Military Experience: A History of the Soviet Army, 1917–1991*, London, UK: Routledge, 2002, p. 167; Rodric Braithwaite, *Afgantsy: The Russians in Afghanistan, 1979–1989*, Oxford, UK: Oxford University Press, 2011, pp. 135, 137; Robert Johnson, *The Afghan Way of War: How and Why They Fight*, Oxford, UK: Oxford University Press, 2011, p. 214; and Thomas Jefferson, *Afghanistan: a Cultural and Political History*, Princeton, NJ: Princeton University Press, 2010, p. 245. The annual desertion rate found in Amtstutz, *Afghanistan: The First Five Years of Soviet Occupation*, p. 181.

269. Hunt, p. 183.

270. "Afghan Forces' Casualties 'Not Sustainable,' U.S. Commander Says."

271. *Ibid.*

272. "U.S. General: Number of Afghan Troop Deaths 'Unsustainable'," United Press International, November 5, 2014, available from *www.upi.com/Top_News/World-News/2014/11/05/US-General-Number-of-Aghan-troop-deaths-unsustainable/6681415223870/*.

273. "Number of ANA Casualties on the Rise," *Tolo News*, October 15, 2014, available from *www.tolonews.com/en/afghanistan/16747-number-of-ana-casualties-on-the-rise*.

274. "MoD: 6853 Afghan Army Soldiers Martyred since 2003," Khaama Press, October 21, 2014, available from *www.khaama.com/mod-6853-afghan-army-soldiers-martyred-since-2003-8857*.

275. *Ibid.*

276. "Afghan Forces' Casualties 'Not Sustainable,' U.S. Commander Says."

277. Catherine Lutz, "US and Coalition Casualties in Iraq and Afghanistan," Providence, Rhode Island: Brown University: Watson Institute, February 21, 2013, Table 4, p. 6, available from *costsofwar.org/sites/default/files/articles/10/attachments/USandCoalition.pdf.*

278. "Quarterly Report to the United States Congress," SIGAR, citing "CSTC-A, response to SIGAR data call, 3/31/2014," p. 97.

279. Lutz, Table 4, p. 6.

280. Approximately 17,867,000 Americans served in the military in World War II. About 39 percent were in rear echelon jobs, roughly double the ANA's 20 percent. Of these, 407,316 were killed and 671,278 were wounded, a total of 1,078,594 KIA and WIA, or 6 percent of all those who served in uniform. Statistics found at the website of the National World War II Museum, available from *www.nationalww2museum.org/learn/education/for-students/ww2-history/ww2-by-the-numbers/us-military.html.*

281. "Afghan Taliban Show Resilience Despite Years of US 'Capture-Kill' Policy," *The Christian Science Monitor*, February 6, 2015, available from *www.csmonitor.com/World/Asia-South-Central/2015/0206/Afghan-Taliban-show-resilience-despite-years-of-US-capture-kill-policy.*

282. "Can Iraq's Fate Befall Afghanistan?" *Al Jazeera*, June 21, 2014, available from *america.aljazeera.com/articles/2014/6/22/afghanistan-can-iraqscrisishappenheretoo.html.*

283. *Ibid.*

284. Gareth Porter, "Tajik Grip on Afghan Army Signals New Ethnic War," IPS, November 20, 2009, available from *ipsnorthamerica.net/print.php?idnews=2707*; Craig Murray, "Civil War Certain as 'Afghan National Army' Now Over 60% Tajik," Craig Murray Blog, March 23, 2010, available from *https://www.craigmurray.org.uk/archives/2010/03/civil_war_certa/.*

285. "Eikenberry Takes Command of Coalition Forces in Afghanistan," *U.S. Department of Defense News*, May 4, 2005, available from *www.defense.gov/news/newsarticle.aspx?id=31741.*

286. Murray, "Civil War Certain as 'Afghan National Army' Now Over 60% Tajik."

287. Louis Dupree, *Afghanistan*, Princeton, NJ: Princeton University Press, 1973; and Sir Olaf Caroë, *The Pathans*, Oxford, UK: Oxford University, 1958.

288. Johnson and Mason, "No Sign until the Burst of Fire."

289. The genealogical veracity of such claims is not important; what is important is that the people themselves hold them as an article of faith.

290. Haroon Rashid, *History of the Pathans*, Vol. 1. Islamabad, Pakistan: Printo Graphic, 2002, p. 83.

291. Charles Kieffer, "Ahmadzi," *Encyclopædia Iranica*. New York: Columbia University, available from *www.iranicaonline.org/ articles/ahmadzi-descendants-of-ahmad-sing*.

292. Thomas Johnson and M. Chris Mason, "Understanding the Taliban and Insurgency in Afghanistan," Philadelphia, PA: Foreign Policy Research Institute, Winter 2007, p. 74.

293. Abdur Rashid Qais, who is said to be the founding father of the Pashtun ethnic group.

294. Caroë, pp. iv, 11-12.

295. Jules Stewart, *The Khyber Rifles: From the British Raj to Al Qaeda*, Stroud, UK: Sutton Publishing, Ltd, 2005.

296. J. A. Robinson, *Notes on Nomad Tribes of Eastern Afghanistan*, New Delhi, India: Government of India Press, 1935.

297. Louis Adamec, ed., *Historical and Political Gazetteer of Afghanistan*, Vols. 1-7. Graz, Austria: Akademische Druck - u. Verlagsanstalt, 1972; Louis Dupree, *Afghanistan*, Princeton, NJ: Princeton University Press, 1973; Henry Priestly, *Afghanistan and its Inhabitants*, Lahore, Pakistan: Sang-e-Meel Publications, 1981. See also *Tribal Hierarchy & Dictionary of Afghanistan*, a reference aid for analysts, McLean, VA: Courage Services, 2007, available from *www.nzdl.org/gsdlmod?e=d-00000-00---off-0areu--00-0----0-10-*

*0---0---0direct-10---4-------0-0l--11-en-50---20-about---00-0-1-00-0-0-11-1-0utfZz-8-00&a=d&c=areu&cl=CL5.9&d=HASH2a85fd9aefbb03 09f2bc86.*

298. Government Accountability Office, "Afghan Army Growing, but Additional Trainers Needed, Long Term Costs not Determined," Washington, DC: U.S. Government Printing Office, January 2011, p. 18.

299. "Efforts to Recruit Pashtuns in Afghan South Falter," *The Wall Street Journal*, September 12, 2010, available from *www.wsj.com/articles/SB10001424052748704621204575487720827425774.*

300. "Tribalism, Governance and Development Workshop Papers," Washington, DC: U.S. Agency for International Development (USAID), July 20, 2010, p. 10, available from *pdf.usaid.gov/pdf_docs/pnaea069.pdf.*

301. Giustozzi, "The Afghan National Army: Sustainability Challenges Beyond Financial Aspects," p. 35.

302. Government Accountability Office, p. 18.

303. At the end of the 19th century, then-Afghan Ruler Abdur Rashid exiled some 10,000 Pashtuns to northern Afghanistan as punishment for defying him, where their descendants live today. Most were assimilated into northern ethnic communities; many became Dari speakers and forgot their Pashtu. Others clustered into villages of primarily Pashtun ethnicity and continue to speak Pashtu. Some number of this small element of Pashtuns living in the north of the country have found their way into the ANA. However, all of the fighting age male Pashtuns living north of the country, together, would not make up even 1 year's recruiting quota for the army.

304. "Public Lecture and Open Discussion 'The Afghan National Army: Sustainability Challenges beyond Financial Aspects'," *ARU*, Tuesday, November 18, 2014, p. 5.

305. Government Accountability Office, "Afghan Army Growing, but Additional Trainers Needed, Long Term Costs not Determined," p. 18.

306. Attributed to Samuel Taylor Coleridge in 1817.

307. Interview with Professor Thomas Johnson, Naval Post-graduate School, Monterey, CA, December 10, 2014.

308. Christian Bleuer, "State-Building, Migration and Economic Development on the Frontiers of Northern Afghanistan and Southern Tajikistan," *Journal of Eurasian Studies*, Vol. 3, Issue 1, January 2012, pp. 69–79.

309. House of Commons: Defence Committee," Securing the Future of Afghanistan: Tenth Report of Session," 2012-13, Vol. 1. London, UK: The Stationary Office Ltd, 2013, Defense Committee Evidence, Ev3.

310. "Paying for the Taliban's Crimes: Abuses against Ethnic Pashtuns in Northern Afghanistan," Human Rights Watch Report, April 2002, Vol. 14, No. 2, available from *www.hrw.org/reports/2002/afghan2/afghan0402.pdf.*

311. Vanda Felbab-Brown, *Aspiration and Ambivalence: Strategies and Realities of Counterinsurgency and State Building in Afghanistan,* Washington, DC: Brookings Institution Press, 2013, p. 57.

312. "Afghanistan in Transition: Crafting a Strategy for Enduring Stability," Beata Górka-Winter and Bartosz Wiśniewski, eds., *Warsaw,* Washington, DC: The Brookings Institute, 2012, available from *www.brookings.edu/~/media/research/files/papers/2012/5/08%20security%20afghanistan%20felbabbrown/08%20security%20afghanistan%20felbabbrown.pdf.*

313. "This is What Winning Looks Like."

314. Murray, "Civil War Certain as 'Afghan National Army' Now Over 60% Tajik."

315. See, for example, "This is What Winning Looks Like."

316. "Instant Justice, Afghan-Army Style, Fails to Win Over Locals," CNN April 12, 2012, available from *www.cnn.com/2012/04/16/world/asia/afghanistan-air-assault/.*

317. "Afghan Army Struggles with Ethnic Divisions," NBC News, July 27, 2010, available from *www.nbcnews.com/id/38432732/ ns/world_news-south_and_central_asia/t/afghan-army-struggles-ethnic-divisions/*.

318. Mohammed Dauran-Ghulam Masum, *Biographies of International Astronauts*, available from *www.spacefacts.de/bios/international/english/dauran_mohammed.htm*.

319. The only officer in the group with less than 100 percent certainty of ethnicity is Brigadier General Dadan Lawang. Lawang replaced Major General Sayed Malouk in December 2014 in command of the 215 Corps during the ongoing crisis in Helmand Province. Lawang's Facebook page is in Dari. He is a 25-year veteran of the Afghan Army, beginning under the Soviets, which virtually ensures he is ethnic Tajik, available from *https://m.facebook.com/GeneralDadanLawang*. Lawang is considered by the Americans to be a rising star in the ANA, having previously been 4th Brigade Commander in 201 Corps and the Commanding Officer of Special Forces Command and a former Commando. However, Lawang is also a Pashto word meaning "clove."

320. "Who is Who in Afghanistan? Mohammadi, Bismillah Khan Muhammadi Bismellah Gen," *Afghan Biographies*, available from *www.afghan-bios.info/index.php?option=com_afghanbios&id=10 68&task=view&total=2981&start=1649&Itemid=2*.

321. Arthur Conan Doyle, *The Adventure of the Beryl Coronet*, Whitefish, MT: Kessinger Publishing, 2005, p. 32.

322. "Drug Problem Adding to Challenge in Afghanistan," *Chicago Tribune*, January 31, 2012.

323. Antonio Giustozzi, "The Afghan National Army: Unwarranted hope?" *RUSI Journal*, Vol. 154, No. 6, 2009, p. 37, available from *www.afghanjirga.net/pdf/ana.pdf*.

324. Paul Lacapruccia, "Another Voice: We are wasting our time and money in Afghanistan," *The Buffalo News*, December 15, 2014.

325. "The Hashish Army—The Afghan National Army," YouTube, 2009, available from *https://www.youtube.com/watch?v=mmU6S_0HVS8*.

326. "This is What Winning Looks Like."

327. "Who Will Pay for Afghan Security Forces?" *Foreign Policy*, June 12, 2014, available from *foreignpolicy.com/2014/06/12/who-will-pay-for-afghan-security-forces/*.

328. *Ibid.*

329. "Afghanistan Economic Update," *The World Bank*, April 2014, available from *www-wds.worldbank.org/external/default/WDSContentServer/WDSP/IB/2014/04/23/000456286_20140423092911/Rendered/PDF/875740WP0Afgha00Box382171B00PUBLIC0.pdf*.

330. "A Decade of Western Aid in Afghanistan—Mission Unsustainable?" *Reuters*, 2014.

331. Steve Sternlieb, "Inadequate Revenue Threatens Afghanistan's Stability," Stability: *International Journal of Security and Development*, 2014, available from *www.stabilityjournal.org/articles/10.5334/sta.dl/*.

332. "Conscription in the Afghan Army: Compulsory Service versus an All-Volunteer Force," Arlington, VA: Center for Naval Analysis, April 2011, pp. 23-24, available from *www.cna.org/sites/default/files/research/CNA%20Conscription%20in%20the%20Afghan%20Army%202%20--%20CRM%20D0024840.A2%20Final.pdf*.

333. Conversation with Rahim Wardak at his home in Kabul, Afghanistan, in May 2002.

334. See *https://www.imf.org/external/np/country/notes/afghanistan.htm*.

335. Kalev Sepp, "Best Practices in Counterinsurgency," *Military Review*, May-June 2005, p. 10.

336. "US Watchdog Warns of Top Seven Threats to Afghan Reconstruction," *The Express Tribune*, December 10, 2014, avail-

able from *tribune.com.pk/story/804934/us-watchdog-warns-of-top-seven-threats- to-afghan-reconstruction/*.

337. "Afghan Army's Rusty Tank Relics Still Roll into Battle," *Stars and Stripes*, July 20, 2014, available from *www.stripes.com/afghan-army-s-rusty-tank-relics-still-roll-into-battle-1.294062*.

338. Ha Mai Viet, *Steel and Blood: South Vietnamese Armor and the War for Southeast Asia*, Monterey, CA: The Naval Institute Press, 2008.

339. See *www.globalsecurity.org/military/world/vietnam/rvn-arvn.htm*.

340. Israeli M-48s met Arab T-55 tanks in battle in the Six Day War in 1967 and had little difficulty defeating them. Samuel Katz and Steven Zaloga, *Tank Battles of the Mid-East Wars 1: The Wars of 1948–1973*, Girardeau, MO: Concord Publishing, 1996. ISBN 978-962-361-612-6.

341. "Army of the Republic of Vietnam (ARVN) - Luc Quon," *Global Security*, available from *www.globalsecurity.org/military/world/vietnam/rvn-arvn.htm*.

342. "Pakistani Government Refused to Move against Radical Madrassas in Punjab," *The Long War Journal*, May 22, 2011, available from *www.longwarjournal.org/archives/2011/05/pakistani_government_2.php*.

343. "Afghan Army Struggles in District Under Siege," *The New York Times*, September 11, 2013, available from *www.nytimes.com/2013/09/12/world/asia/afghan-army-struggles-in-district-under-siege.html?pagewanted=all*.

344. "Taliban Press for Advantage as Politicians Work on Maneuvers in Kabul," *The New York Times*, September 28, 2014, available from *www.nytimes.com/2014/09/29/world/asia/taliban-presses-for-advantage-as-politicians-work-on-maneuvers-in-kabul.html*.

345. "Guide to the Analysis of Insurgency," p. 12.

346. Johnson, *The Afghan Way of War*.

347. *Ibid.*

348. "Taliban Overrun an Afghan Army Base."

349. "Taliban Push into Afghan Districts that U.S. Had Secured."

# PART II:

## AFGHANISTAN YEAR-BY-YEAR 2015-19

We have an issue with the will of the Iraqis to fight [ISIS] and defend themselves. We can give them training, we can give them equipment; we obviously can't give them the will to fight.[1]

U.S. Secretary of Defense Ashton Carter

## MOTIVATION: WHY THE AFGHAN NATIONAL ARMY WILL COLLAPSE IN THE SOUTH

One, two, three, what are we fighting for?[2]

1960s anti-war song, "Feel like I'm Fixin' to Die" by Country Joe McDonald

This part describes, year-by-year, what will happen in Afghanistan from 2015 to 2019 and why, using the available statistics and comparable outcomes of Vietnam and Iraq and a spectrum of unclassified Afghan indicators. It examines the key reasons for the collapse of the Army of the Republic of Vietnam (ARVN) and the Iraqi Army, and the pending collapse of the Afghan National Army (ANA) in the south of Afghanistan. As shown in Part I, with almost no combat power, the Afghan National Police (ANP) will not be a military factor (see Appendix II).

All three states — South Vietnam, Iraq, and Afghanistan — collapsed or will collapse because their U.S.-built armies collapsed, but this alone does not explain why all three states have turned out so differently from the democracies envisioned by U.S. policymakers. In fact, the collapse of South Vietnam and Iraq and the inevitable collapse of Afghanistan were ultimately not the failures of the U.S. Army, or of the U.S. military and Navy in general. The cause lies much deeper than armies, navies, and air forces.

The armies of South Vietnam and Iraq collapsed almost immediately when confronted with military force. The ARVN ceased organized resistance within 6 weeks of a North Vietnamese Army (NVA) armored reconnaissance in force entering South Vietnamese territory, although it was qualitatively and quantitatively superior on paper.[3] We will dispense here and now with the trendy but ahistorical revisionist claim that the ARVN lost because the U.S. Congress cut ARVN funding. This simply never happened, and this falsehood has been comprehensively debunked.[4] Congress **never** stopped funding support to South Vietnam. This misinformation was started by Melvin Laird in 2005 in a blatantly dishonest attempt to re-write history. In fact, funding to the ARVN continued to the last day of South Vietnam, and the ARVN had warehouses full of ammunition and materiel when it surrendered. No serious academic historian of the Vietnam War accepts this deliberate lie.[5]

The Iraqi army's cohesion in the face of a determined offensive by a small force of irregulars can be measured in hours. When a few hundred Islamic State of Iraq and Syria (ISIS) militiamen attacked Mosul, for example, the 30,000-man Iraqi army garrison there fled, shedding their uniforms and equipment as they ran.[6] After the departure of U.S. advisors, there is no reason to suggest the ANA, with half as many men and roughly twice as much territory to defend as the Iraqi Army, will fare significantly better. What caused these armies to collapse? As this part of the book will demonstrate, all three collapsed or will collapse for the same reasons. Indeed, the failure of all three was predictable, even inevitable, to dispassionate and objective political analysts. Furthermore, this was clear before the first local soldier entered basic training, not in hindsight but in foresight. What lessons should have been learned from Vietnam? What lessons should now be learned again from the current military re-intervention in Iraq and the crisis in Afghanistan?

Warfare is a conflict of moral purposes. In war, as Napoleon noted, "the moral [i.e., motivation to fight] is to the physical [i.e., force size] as three is to one."[7] Carl von Clausewitz, too, emphasized the importance of the moral (motivational) aspect of war: "The moral forces are amongst the most important in war," Clausewitz wrote, adding they constitute "the Will which puts in motion and guides the whole mass of powers, uniting [them] . . . in one stream. . . . The value of the moral powers, and their frequently incredible influence, are best exemplified by history."[8] The most serious deficit of the Afghan National Security Forces (ANSF) is not its lack of an air force, extreme over-reliance on weak and static police forces, small size, nonexistent logistics, pervasive drug abuse, or the attrition that runs near 50 percent per year in combat units in the south, none of which substantively afflicted the ARVN to anywhere near the severity of these problems in the ANSF today. It is its lack of motivation in comparison to the Taliban.

Although there are exceptions, there is simply a general lack of will in the ANSF to fight the Taliban in the south at the soldier and policeman level. As Afghan War veteran and military analyst John Cook notes:

Additional trainers are not enough to turn the situation around if there is no will to win from the Afghans. The truth is the Afghan army is not very good and they won't fight. This is where we are after ten years and billions of dollars invested in training and equipping them with state of the art technology and weapons . . . the Taliban, lacking any formal military training, poorly led and poorly equipped, often living in caves, enduring incredible hardships, shows far more fight and aggressiveness on the battlefield than the Afghan army . . . the Taliban believe in their cause enough to die for it, while the Afghan [army] soldiers do not. . . .This behavior can be traced directly to a lack of national identity and national loyalty. Nor do they have a cause they are willing to die for. . . . They are in the army for one reason only: for the money.[9]

The International Security Assistance Force (ISAF) attempted to control the discourse of ANA performance over the past decade with an amplified narrative of positive ANA operations, but the truth consistently leaks through in press and military reporting. In fact, the reports of this lack of fighting motivation and morale failure in the ANA are pervasive and consistent. Even when partnered with Americans, the ANA lacks fighting spirit. During the fight for Combat Outpost (COP) Keating in 2009, for example, known as the Battle of Kamdesh, ANA soldiers hid under their beds or looted the American barracks.[10] As one American combat advisor noted:

In Afghanistan, the problem we had training the ANA was that they only really gave a shit about themselves and their tribal group. Northern Pashtuns were especially bad with this. I caught a group of them smoking hash when they were supposed to be patrolling and their commander gave them a tongue lashing, but they really didn't understand why they should be in-

132

terested in Afghan security as a whole versus just their own village/family/friends.[11]

American troops are not the only ones reporting systemic ANA failure to fight. Latvian advisors stationed at COP Keating told U.S. investigators the Afghan soldiers lacked "discipline, motivation, and initiative."[12] Decorated British soldier Doug Beattie notes the ANA "refused to fight" and lacked fighting spirit during the British campaign around Garmsir in Helmand Province.[13] British Captain Mike Martin wrote of the British campaign in Helmand that "the Afghan army in Helmand was nonexistent. The local Afghan police were, on the whole, criminal."[14]

During the fighting around Marjah in 2010, Marines reported the ANA lacked motivation, refused to carry out their duties, and spent their time looting the bazaar and smoking hashish.[15] An embedded reporter with the 2nd Brigade Combat Team, 101st Airborne, in Zhari district in 2010 described the ANA unit that the American troopers were operating with, the 4th Company, 3rd Brigade, 205 Corps, as "clueless and stoned." During one firefight, the reporter observed:

few soldiers . . . seemed even to know how to fire their weapons properly. . . . As insurgent gunfire spat overhead, some soldiers stared listlessly at the sky, their hands pressed to their ears. Others crawled among the vines, huddling among the roots, dazed and disorientated, their weapons useless in their hands. . . . Their machine gunners had left most of their ammunition behind. They refused to provide sentries, or else slept at their posts. . . . Befuddled on hash, one machine gunner dozed off, oblivious to the firefight around him. A junior officer appeared briefly to chastise another group of troops for getting stoned, before he too wandered off and fell asleep, ignored by his men

. . . . The company commander seemed to be in hiding for most of the operation while one of their platoon commanders . . . simply walked away from his men as he beat a retreat for the safety of a compound. One of the enlisted 101st Airborne troopers said 'Look at that one,' pointing out an ANA soldier who wandered down a vineyard track in the midst of the shooting, glassy-eyed, without any weapon. 'I don't know what it is with this unit, but they are worse than useless. . . . They are a complete liability'.[16]

An Army soldier named Andrew Carson shared COP Pirtle-King in Kunar province for a year with three different Afghan National Army platoons, observing that:

> the majority of the ANA we dealt with were poorly trained, lacked discipline, and were cowards. . . . They didn't want our help or training. It seemed that they really didn't care about their own country. We found out that one of the platoon sergeants was getting paid by the Taliban to give them information about our movements and fire missions. He was detained and sent to Bagram. We had one of the Afghan soldiers 'accidentally' shoot one of our M240 machine-gunners in the leg. A lot of the soldiers lacked discipline while on missions which endangered everyone with them, and a number of them would fall out of foot patrols after just half a click.[17]

Based on what he saw, Carson concluded that "Afghanistan will follow the path that Iraq has, but with less of a fight."[18] A former Battalion Sergeant Major of the North Carolina National Guard who deployed to Afghanistan put it more succinctly: "The ANA is not worth a shit," he said, adding "there is no sense of nation or nationality in Afghanistan by the Afghan people."[19] Former U.S. Army War College (USAWC)

Commandant Major General Robert Scales (Retired) believes that "when we leave, the ANA will scatter like leaves in a stiff breeze."[20]

Fighting spirit has not improved over time. U.S. Army Sergeant First Class Keith Norris, who served as a combat advisor to the ANA in Paktika province, wrote in 2012 in *Military Review* that "American soldiers consistently view their Afghan counterparts as untrustworthy, unmotivated, and inept."[21] During the fighting in Helmand in 2013, according to *The New York Times*, "The Afghan soldiers seldom leave the installation, and mostly refuse to conduct missions — too dangerous, they say . . . American officers admit the ANA has an 'addiction to bases'."[22] Antonio Giustozzi noted in February 2014 that the motivation of the ANA "rank and file" to fight was "dubious."[23] In June 2014, Special Forces (SFs) operating with ANA personnel in Zabul province reported the same pattern of behavior, including ANA soldiers refusing to help form a secure perimeter and "huddling behind rocks" during the fighting.[24] *The New York Times* described ANA performance in Helmand that summer as "lackluster."[25]

By the end of the fighting season in 2014, the *Times* said, "the cowed Afghan Army unit [in Sangin] was mostly unwilling to leave its base to confront the threat. Late last year, reports of a deal between a local army commander and the Taliban began to surface."[26] In October, *The Economist* described ANA morale as "low," noting that many soldiers had not been paid for months.[27] On November 29, 2014, the Taliban overran the ANA garrison in Sangin, killing 14 ANA soldiers. Another six or seven were missing in action. The ANA forces in the Sangin District Center 300 yards away from the ANA garrison did not sortie to counterattack and relieve their comrades, instead firing in the dark over the walls of their fort in the general direction of the garrison.[28] Former Marine and former Assistant Secretary of Defense Bing West, who served in the Combined Action Platoon (CAP) program in Vietnam and spent months with Marines in Helmand province, corroborates the poor morale and poor fighting qualities of the ANA as well as U.S. Marines' low regard for them across the board.[29] West also noted that, while he and thousands of other Marines lived with their Vietnamese counterparts in rural villages in Vietnam, no American forces would ever live with their Afghan counterparts because of the extremely high risk of betrayal.[30]

Few military leaders would dispute the principle that troops with high morale and strong motivation are better and more aggressive fighters than those without. Here again, Afghanistan resembles Vietnam. There are remarkable parallels between the certainty of victory among the enemies of the state in Vietnam, Iraq, and Afghanistan. In each case, the enemy's will to fight overall was greater than that of their opponents. In the case of Vietnam, a senior advisor on the Phoenix program to neutralize Viet Cong cadre, Colonel Jack Weissinger, interviewed hundreds of known mid-level Viet Cong officials and recorded that:

> One of the underlying beliefs I have, and it is unshakeable by the way, is that there was a basic difference, possibly in the cultural background, possibly in the people, but certainly in the motivation of the North Vietnamese and Viet Cong, on one hand, and the followers of the [Government of South Vietnam] GVN on the other . . . I was struck, time and again, with the terribly strong belief they had in what they were doing. They absolutely believed, and I mean every one of them, that they were going to win eventually.

They didn't believe in a military victory at that time, I don't think any of them did, but they all believed in the inevitable, final, political victory or combination military-political victory. That was a universal belief with them. It was right down inside the skin, they believed it so strongly.[31]

As former Secretary of Defense Robert McNamara noted with hindsight and understatement in 1996:

We underestimated the power of nationalism to motivate people (in this case, the North Vietnamese and the Viet Cong) to fight and die for their beliefs and values — and we continue to do so today in many parts of the world.[32]

A parallel motivational dynamic is at work in Afghanistan today in relation to the Taliban. According to a British Broadcasting Corporation report in February 2012, confirmed by NATO's International Security Assistance Force (ISAF) in Afghanistan and the U.S. Department of Defense, interviews with thousands of Taliban detainees over a period of many years are unequivocal empirical evidence that the Taliban are utterly dedicated to battlefield victory, uninterested in any negotiated settlement, and absolutely confident of the final victory of their cause. In the NATO report, confirmed and acknowledged by both Lieutenant Colonel Jimmie Cummings, a spokesman for ISAF in Afghanistan and U.S. Department of Defense spokesman Captain (now Rear Admiral) John Kirby, "the Taliban are absolutely confident of victory, based on 27,000 interviews with over 4,000 detainees ranging from senior Taliban commanders to Afghan civilians. They also include mid- and low-level Taliban, al-Qaeda, and foreign fighters." Lieutenant Colonel Cummings publicly authenticated the information in the report, which he confirmed in a press conference represented the "opinions or ideals" of Taliban detainees.[33] Then-Captain Kirby, in publicly discussing the document at a press conference in February 2012, confirmed that the report, called "State of the Taliban 2012," is "the product of thousands of interviews with Taliban detainees in 2011." Appearing before the U.S. Senate Select Committee on Intelligence one day earlier, on January 31, 2012, the Director of National Intelligence James Clapper confirmed that the Taliban "remains a resilient, determined adversary."[34]

In Vietnam, Iraq, and Afghanistan, U.S. military officers dismissed the importance of these findings, confident of the superiority of American troops, tactics, commitment, and equipment. This confidence was not misplaced; in all three conflicts, the American Soldier was a better fighter than any of his opponents. However, in all three wars, the confidence of higher-ranking American military officers and advisors in the fighting potential of their respective **local** troops and senior-level American enthusiasm for their performance was, and is, misplaced. Scales recently referred to this subjective bias toward the ANA on the part of U.S. trainers as "spin."[35] This is another similarity to the Vietnam War, according to historian Arnold Isaacs. Isaacs argues that the Richard Nixon administration embarked on a large and far-reaching information campaign to make "failure look like success," beginning with Nixon's famous "silent majority" speech.[36]

A report prepared in January 2014 by the Department of Defense (DoD) concluded that not only does the ANA lack motivation, the Afghan civilian population in many parts of Afghanistan are also sure the Taliban eventually will win, according to CNN:

... dramatic increases in fighting against the Taliban have failed to convince the local population that the Afghan government and coalition forces will succeed. 'The Taliban's strength lies in the Afghan population's perception that Coalition forces will soon leave, giving credence to the belief that a Taliban victory is inevitable,' the report says.[37]

In Iraq, too, the Iraqi Army lacked the will to fight, even briefly, despite overwhelming quantitative and qualitative superiority. The opponents of the Iraqi Army, the terrorist group ISIS, have a similar level of fanatical motivation to that of the Viet Cong, the NVA, and the Taliban. One ISIS terrorist noted: "I think it's impossible that the new [Iraqi] army can defeat ISIS." The Mosul-based terrorist added: "The [ISIS] gunmen are highly trained. They are ready to sacrifice their lives to get what they want and they are motivated by religion."[38] In comparison, the Iraqi governor of Nineveh province, Atheel al Nujaifi, says of the Iraqi Army, "the leaders and the soldiers have no military experience and have no convictions."[39]

One of the primary lessons unlearned from Vietnam, Iraq, and Afghanistan is that soldiers in the armies we create, train, and equip are simply not willing to fight and die for the weak, corrupt, illegitimate governments that we stand up in parallel, no matter how big they are or how much equipment we give them. As McNamara admitted in 1996, Vietnam War planners:

> ... failed to adhere to the fundamental principle that, in the final analysis, if the South Vietnamese were to be saved, they had to win the war for themselves. . . .We viewed the people and leaders of South Vietnam in terms of our own experience. We saw in them a thirst for—and a determination to fight for—freedom and

democracy. We totally misjudged the political forces within the country.[40]

The ARVN that the United States created collapsed in 6 weeks, and the Iraqi Army that the United States created collapsed in 6 hours because they had neither a national sense of country nor a government — in Saigon or Baghdad — that its soldiers believed was worth dying for. The ANA will certainly not fare any better than the ARVN or the Iraqi Army (IA) after we leave, and for the very same reason.

## WHERE DOES MOTIVATION COME FROM? THE CRITICAL LEGITIMACY FACTOR

The cafes of Vienna might seem an unlikely place to find a preeminent source of military wisdom. Yet, it was there 100 years ago that the father of modern sociology, Karl "Max" Weber, did his seminal work on legitimacy of governance, *Politik als Beruf*.[41] Weber famously identified three basic sources of governmental legitimacy, which he characterized as traditional, charismatic, and rational-legal.[42] Traditional legitimacy originates in social cultures that historically respect the authority of tradition. In this group, Weber included dynastic, hereditary leadership — monarchies and patriarchal systems — which included segmentary tribal organizations like the Pashtuns. Charismatic leadership, Weber writes, is the human response to the personal charisma of a person or an idea. Weber included religious authority in this category. "Religious" leadership is self-explanatory, but would obviously include, for example, as archetypes the former Caliphate of Islam and the Papacy of Catholic Europe in the Middle Ages.[43] The terrorist organization ISIS in Iraq and Syria today seeks to claim legitimacy to rule by proclaiming itself as the new caliphate for the Muslim world, and indeed has attracted recruits from all over the world with the power of this perceived legitimacy.[44] Taliban leader *Mullah* Omar obtained the same legitimacy by donning the sacred Cloak of the Prophet in Kandahar in 1996 and proclaiming himself the *Amir ul-Mumaneen*, or leader of the faithful.[45] (In Central Asian culture, such articles of clothing convey enormous authority as they are believed to literally embody the power and sanctity of the original wearer.[46]) Rational-legal legitimacy comes from a system of institutional procedure, wherein government institutions establish order through the consent of the governed. Weber included in this category all of the forms of representative government that the democracies of Europe and North America today embody, and that have in common a basis in the rule of law and elective popular representation. This is the **source of legitimacy** of all western governments today.

The nucleus of the U.S. failures in South Vietnam, Iraq, and Afghanistan was the political failure to have any legitimacy of governance. Despite the fact that none of the three countries ever had any experience of Weber's third source of legitimacy, i.e., democracy and government institutions that established social order through the consent of the governed, the United States attempted to impose one in each country anyway, and deliberately excluded any other source of legitimacy.

Without exception, for 2,000 years, Afghanistan has known only the first two of these sources. Afghanistan has been ruled by kings, emirs, and empires, including the Samanids and the Seljuk Turks, whose rule over what today is Afghanistan was endorsed by

Abbasid Caliphs in Baghdad (in other words, traditional legitimacy **reinforced** by charismatic legitimacy).[47] Afghanistan, for all intents and purposes, has no experience at all with the third source of legitimacy of governance, i.e., democracy, the rule of law, and representative government. The international community, in the form of the United States and the United Nations, led by Lakhdar Brahimi and allied with a tiny group of educated, expatriate, urban Kabuli elites, entered the medieval rural Afghan world of traditional and religious legitimacy in 2001 and 2002 with the so-called Bonn Process.[48] Working together with one or two idealistic western scholars who shared the patently false view of this handful of educated, westernized Afghan urban elites that Afghanistan was ready for democracy, the ideologically neo-conservative U.S. Government created a new Afghan polity that comprehensively eliminated or marginalized the only two culturally acceptable sources of government legitimacy, the **traditional** and the **religious**. Here the United States again forgot not only the wisdom of General Douglas MacArthur regarding land forces in Asia but also his lessons from post-war Japan. MacArthur knew the Japanese people and culture,[49] and he recognized that the beloved Japanese Emperor was a critical symbol of national unity for a defeated nation. MacArthur ensured the Emperor would **remain** as a ceremonial figurehead, in a role much like the monarchy of the United Kingdom (UK).[50]

The monarchy in Afghanistan, although it had been in exile since 1973, nevertheless remained enormously popular with the Afghan people[51] and conveyed among them the critical **traditional** legitimacy of governance that Weber described. When King Zahir Shah spoke to the Afghan people on the radio a few days after the attacks of September 11, 2001, "I almost cried," said one young man in Kabul, "you can't believe how reassuring it was just to hear his voice." The day after the King's address, the value of the national currency doubled. There was literally dancing in the streets. "All the ethnic groups in Afghanistan support Zahir Shah — Pashtuns, Tajiks, Uzbeks, and Hazaras," the BBC quoted another man as saying. "All the other leaders and the armed factions couldn't bring peace and stability, but he will," said a third man. "Yes, we'll welcome him," said a fourth, "when he was our ruler, our king, we had hunger, but we had peace." As the BBC correspondent noted, "It is actually quite difficult to find an Afghan who does not want the former king back."[52] Despite the blatant obviousness of the return of the King in a largely ceremonial role as the one chance Afghanistan now had for peace and stability, the United States abolished the monarchy via proxies, against the express wishes of 75 percent of the official delegates to the Emergency Loya Jirga in 2002, who signed a petition requesting King Zahir Shah be made the interim leader of Afghanistan.[53] The Central Intelligence Agency (CIA) subverted this petition[54] and had Zalmay Khalilzad browbeat the elderly king into abdicating his throne.[55] As United Press International (UPI) reported at the time, "After nearly 25 years of war, democracy nearly broke out in Afghanistan on Monday, but was blocked by backroom dealing to prevent former King Mohammed Zahir Shah from emerging as a challenger to Hamid Karzai, head of the current interim government."[56]

Into this void of political legitimacy in 2002 returned the Taliban with its **religious** source of legitimacy to fill the vacuum. It had to be one or the other, the monarchy or Islam, because the third source (legal) has no legitimacy in Afghanistan. The Taliban today only have the support of one-third of the Afghan people,[57] but they are seen as legitimate, which should not be conflated with popularity. Leaders can be seen as the legitimate leaders of their countries without being popular, as American presidents from Abraham Lincoln to Barack Obama know only too well. The Bonn Process coupled this illegitimacy of democracy to a system of strong central authority, which Afghanistan has never accepted. In short, in Afghanistan, the United States attempted to create something that has never existed successfully, a strong central government, based on a source of legitimacy that has never existed, democracy, by implementing a strategy of "extending the reach of the central government," which for a thousand years has always provoked a virulent, rural, conservative insurgency based in Islamic models of resistance.[58] At a critical inflection point in Afghanistan's history, it was a catastrophic western diplomatic failure at the Bonn conference, not military failure, that sealed Afghanistan's fate. After the abolition of the monarchy and the de jure establishment of a highly centralized state government that gave no power to the regions, to the King or to the *mullahs*, there was simply **never** any chance of a successful outcome.

The same fundamental mistake was repeated in South Vietnam, Iraq, and Afghanistan. In each case, the United States removed unpopular leaders who were perceived to have some legitimacy to govern (Diem, Hussein, and *Mullah* Omar) and replaced them with unpopular leaders who were illegitimate (Thieu, al Maliki, and Karzai). In each case, grown men and women in the United States actually operated under the belief that, in primitive countries with no experience of democracy, entire populations could be transformed virtually overnight into Jeffersonian democrats. The operating assumption was apparently that, when the people of each country somehow instinctively recognized the inherent superiority of western democracy over whatever they had been doing for the last thousand years, they would, in a forehead-slapping moment of epiphany, suddenly be enraptured by democracy and believe it to be legitimate. But the simple fact is that elections do not make democracies, democracies make elections. As retired CIA senior analyst Paul Pillar recently noted:

> The cause of the political crisis in Afghanistan is . . . to be found . . . in the lack of a political culture that nurtures the habits of thought and behavior critical to the smooth functioning of a stable democracy [including] . . . fairness, inclusiveness, and observance of impartial rules — and confidence that one's political opponents are displaying those habits as well. A failure to recognize the importance of a democratic political culture . . . and the time it takes to develop one has led repeatedly to the mistaken belief that in a troubled country (be it Afghanistan, Ukraine, Iraq, South Vietnam, or someplace else), if we just pick the right leader and give him enough support, including at times military support, stable democracy will prevail.[59]

All the military effort in South Vietnam, Iraq and Afghanistan was futile, because politically, in Saigon, Baghdad, and Kabul, there was, and is, no perception of a legitimate government that had, or has, the support of the rural population and for which the people were willing to fight. It is the rural population in Afghanistan that matters, as Giustozzi notes, because virtually all the recruits in the ANA are from rural hamlets.[60] In another critical parallel between South

145

Vietnam and Afghanistan, one of the Vietnam War's best historians, Eric Bergerud, has written that:

> The . . . GVN lacked legitimacy with the rural peasantry, the largest segment of the population. . . . The peasantry perceived the GVN to be aloof, corrupt, and inefficient . . . South Vietnam's urban elite possessed the outward manifestations of a foreign culture . . . more importantly, this small group held most of the wealth and power in a poor nation, and the attitude of the ruling elite toward the rural population was, at best, paternalistic and, at worst, predatory.[61]

As Jeffrey Record notes, "the fundamental political obstacle to an enduring American success in Vietnam [was] a politically illegitimate, militarily feckless, and thoroughly corrupted South Vietnamese client regime."[62] Like Afghanistan, South Vietnam at the government level was a massively corrupt collection of self-interested warlords, many of them deeply implicated in the profitable opium trade—including in both Vietnam and Afghanistan, the President's own brother—with almost nonexistent loyalty outside the capital city beyond that which could be bought with bribery, patronage, and corruption. The purely military gains achieved at such terrible cost in our nation's blood and treasure in Vietnam, Afghanistan, and Iraq never came close to exhausting the enemy's manpower pool or his will to fight, and simply could not be sustained politically by illegitimate and dysfunctional state institutions where corrupt self-interest at every level from the minister to the desk clerk was and is the sole order of the day. As McNamara writes, "external military force cannot substitute for the political order and stability that must be forged by a people for themselves."[63] In other words, the military cannot provide a national identity. Nixon's "Vietnamization" of that conflict, President George W. Bush's "Iraqification" of the Iraq War, and President Obama's "Afghanization" of the Afghan War were never sustainable. As the Joint Chiefs of Staff warned Secretary of State John Foster Dulles in 1954, "Strong and stable governments and societies are necessary to support the creation of strong armies."[64] Vietnam, Iraq, and Afghanistan were a century away from having either one.

## THE FALLACY OF "NATION-BUILDING"

"Nation-building" is frequently conflated with "state-building." It is, in political terms, a fluid concept that has been given multiple definitions over time by many political scientists. The definitions of nation-building and state-building themselves are the subjects of ongoing debates and semantic arguments, and the topic has generated a large volume of academic literature.[65] As Carolyn Stephenson notes, "Nation-building is a normative concept that means different things to different people."[66] Paul Beinart for example, defines nation-building as "the use of armed force in the aftermath of a crisis to promote a transition to democracy."[67] This is essentially the same definition contrived by James Dobbins as: "the use of armed force in the aftermath of a conflict to underpin an enduring transition to democracy."[68] For the purposes of this book, however, nation-building simply refers to the evolutionary process of creating and establishing a broad, deep, and pervasive personal sense of national identity in a great majority of the population, rather than one that is centered in a localized identity: "I am a German" for example, as opposed to "I am a Bavarian"; or "I am an American" as opposed to "I am a Catholic" or "I am a Latino." It is about creating a sense of primary personal identity that is located at the level of the nation, rather than one grounded first in region, race, religion, tribe, language, culture, or political affiliation. As Godfrey Mwakikagile writes, "Tribalism is incompatible with nationalism, and nation-building is impossible without nationhood. And you can't have nationhood without a genuine feeling of common citizenship and identity."[69]

Higher levels of identity can be achieved as nations mature. The current political experiment of the European Union (EU) is an excellent example of how nations may seek to transcend national identities to begin to forge larger regional identities based on shared values and economic interests. As the struggles of the EU to create workable political and economic policies demonstrate, however, this is not an easy process. But beyond any reasonable doubt, becoming a nation is a necessary precursor stage of state maturity through which all countries must pass before transcending this 18th century concept. Tribal and sectarian societies cannot leap-frog nationhood to democracy. It has never been done. Nor does nationhood always ensure unity or stability: The cases of the Basques in Spain and Scotland's independence movement in the UK are examples of the persistence of sub-national fissures within modern, developed nations.

A state is properly defined as the governmental apparatus by which a country rules itself. Max Weber provided the classic definition of the state:

> Today, however, we have to say that a state is a human community that (successfully) claims the monopoly of the legitimate use of physical force within a given territory. Note that territory is one of the characteristics of the state. Specifically, at the present time, the right to use physical force is ascribed to other institutions

or to individuals only to the extent to which the state permits it.[70]

By this definition, Afghanistan is neither a state nor a nation.

State-**building**, therefore, refers to building or reinforcing the institutions of civil society. These might include fostering more transparent voting procedures, for example, or supporting society-state relations in the justice, education, or health care sectors. The interrelationship between nationhood and state-building is complex. Having a national identity can itself be nuanced and subtle in mature nations. In the case of Switzerland, for example, three major ethnic groups speaking four national languages live in 26 cantons, each of which has its own constitution. Yet, there is a national army, in which all males serve, a national government, and a single currency, and the people of Switzerland think of themselves as Swiss regardless of which canton they are from. Switzerland has existed since 1291, last having been involved in a war more than 200 years ago. It has almost no natural resources, yet it is prosperous, and civil unrest is virtually unknown.

Afghanistan, in contrast, has only two official languages (and more than 60 unofficial ones) and three major ethnic groups (defined as comprising more than 10 percent of the population), vast mineral resources, and mountainous terrain similar to Switzerland. Yet the overwhelming majority of Afghans live in desperate poverty, have no sense of national identity, and have rarely, if ever, known peace, education, or justice. After 13 years of American engagement, Afghanistan in 2014 set an all-time record on the *Gallup World Poll* human suffering index.[71] Already the worst in the world, Afghan suffering in 2014 reached a global historical high.[72] In July 2014, U.S. reconstruction spending in Afghanistan exceeded the Marshall Plan,[73] yet, despite the United States spending $3,350 for every man, woman, and child in Afghanistan since 2002,[74] it remains the poorest country in the world. As journalist Anna Corsaro notes, "Absolute poverty has risen by about 10 percentage points in Afghanistan since the beginning of the war; life expectancy has fallen to 44 years, [and] infant mortality has increased to reach 150 per thousand."[75] Not surprisingly, on November 18, 2014, John Sopko, the Special Inspector General for Afghanistan Reconstruction (SIGAR), termed the entire Afghan reconstruction effort "an abysmal failure."[76] What accounts for the difference? Switzerland is a nation, Afghanistan is not.

U.S. foreign policy is relatively uncomplicated regarding developed and developing democracies that are at peace and do not harbor international terrorists. We trade with them and, in the latter case, attempt to provide aid in the form of civilian-led programs designed to foster the state-building process. More recently, military cooperation has morphed into a major component of American foreign policy. Prior to World War II, the United States did not participate in multinational training exercises or provide any peacetime armaments or training to foreign countries. Since the Vietnam War, in particular, the U.S. military has positioned itself as a major component of state-building ostensibly limited to the sector of national defense and state security.

After World War II, what the United States did in Japan and Germany was **state**-building, not nation-building. Both the Germans and the Japanese **already** had a strong sense of national identity, indeed a highly militarized national identity. Both had developed economies, functioning justice systems, high literacy levels, and pervasive civil order enforced by (however repugnant and unacceptable their methods) relatively corruption-free professional policing. The challenge was building enduring democratic institutions, not creating a national identity. Germany had experience of democracy in the Weimar Republic and a highly literate population; Japan had its beloved Emperor to sustain it through the transition. Seventy years later, the United States still has substantial numbers of troops stationed in both countries.

After the Korean War, the United States faced a different challenge. Korea was not a defeated enemy, but an ally that had helped fight its way back from the brink of extinction to a delicate cessation of hostilities in which both North and South remained heavily armed and ideologically opposed. No peace treaty has ever been signed.[77] The Koreans on the south of the Demilitarized Zone (DMZ), like their northern brothers and sisters, were largely illiterate, poor, and underdeveloped. They did, however, have a common ethnicity, and they shared a common language and religion. The sense of being Korean as a primary identity was nearly universal. They were already a **nation**. The challenges here, too, were **state**-building, and transforming a sense of national political identity into being specifically democratic **South** Korean as distinct from being (communist) North Korean. This task was complicated by the multitude of family ties that reached across the DMZ. Success was not easy, nor did it come quickly. Post-war Korea experienced significant political turmoil, going through six periods, or republics, before emerging in the 21st century as a liberal democracy.[78] The first of these, formed in 1945 after the surrender of Japan and known as the First Republic under Syngman Rhee, was staunchly anti-communist and was in place for 5 years before the outbreak of the Korean War.[79] This continuity provided significant advantages in state-building after the hostilities ended, despite Syngman Rhee's shortcomings as an (increasingly) authoritarian ruler.[80] Nevertheless, even given nationhood and these other advantages, stable liberal democracy and middle class prosperity took nearly 70 years to emerge, following periods of military rule, and, of course, the United States has maintained a sizeable garrison in the country since the end of World War II. During these 70 years, a more nuanced sense of national identity in the sense of being a **South** Korean has indeed emerged without diminishing a larger sense of being one people and a continuing desire for peaceful reunification with the North. Today the South Korean (Republic of Korea [ROK]) Army is both powerful and imbued with an aggressive spirit and an intense will to fight. The author served in Korea and operated with the ROK Army and Marine Corps, and has never heard a U.S. military officer speak disparagingly about either.

All countries are different, and each is unique. It would be reductionist and simplistic to suggest that what worked in one country will work in another. Nevertheless, certain larger, strategic, historical lessons can be drawn that should inform foreign policy. The first of these is that state-building takes a long time. Success in Germany, Japan, and Korea came about slowly during significant and unbroken 70-year U.S. military defense treaty commitments, a large U.S. force presence, and sustained economic investment. In the cases of Germany and Japan, the latter took the form of the Marshall Plan.

The futile U.S. effort at nation-creation and concurrent state-building in South Vietnam, in contrast, lasted 12 years; the attempt in Iraq, 10 years; while the effort in Afghanistan has ground on for 13 years. Even these durations are misleading; the rotation of military officers and civilian officials every 6 to 12 months meant that little expertise was accumulated, and little traction was sustained anywhere. As Army officer and U.S. Agency for International Development official John Paul Vann famously said of America's experience in Vietnam, "We don't have 12 years' experience in Vietnam. We have 1 year's experience 12 times."[81] The same is true in equal measure of Iraq and Afghanistan. The government left in place in South Vietnam lasted 3 years; the government left behind in Iraq lasted just 2 years. How long the government left in place after the withdrawal of all U.S. forces from Afghanistan (whenever that happens) endures is predictable. Given its complete lack of nationhood; its complete lack of legitimacy of governance; its unworkable "unity government"; its geostrategic location; its innumerable ethnic, sectarian, and linguistic fissures; the current Taliban war against the government; its completely inadequate and unmotivated security forces; its imploding economy and its perpetual status as a pawn in a larger game between India, Iran, and Pakistan—the 2 to 3 years of Iraq and South Vietnam, respectively, are a reasonable projection. The Soviet-backed regime of President Mohammad Najibullah also lasted 3 years after the collapse of the Soviet Union and the resulting cutoff of Soviet funding. What would be unreasonable would be to think that Afghanistan—with all the ethnic and sectarian hatreds of Iraq, multiplied by all the poverty and rural isolation of South Vietnam—will fare better than either did after our departure. The strategic reason for this is that all three are not **nations**. They were not yet or are not yet "nation-built."

Succinctly put, nation-building is impossible. This is the single most important lesson unlearned from Vietnam, Iraq, and Afghanistan. As historian Jeffrey Clark notes, no nation, no matter how powerful, has the capacity to "reform and reshape the society of another."[82] There are no successful examples in our history of nation-building. As Secretary of Defense Chuck Hagel, himself a Vietnam combat veteran with the Purple Heart, recently noted:

> I learned as I walked through this 12 months of war in 1968 . . . you cannot impose your will, you cannot impose your values, you cannot impose your standards, your institutions on other societies in other countries. It has never worked. Never will work.[83]

The United States has never occupied a country with troops and camped out long enough for the slow, evolutionary, internally driven social process of becoming a nation to occur. How long this process might take, under full military occupation and with complete enforced control over the building blocks of education, justice, and honest policing, as was done in the Philippines after the Spanish-American War, for example, is difficult to say. There are no precedents. The U.S. experiment in social engineering in the Philippines was terminated by the Japanese Imperial Army in 1942, and the insurgency today in Mindanao and smaller southern islands rages on, despite the fact that the Philippines largely meet the test of being a nation. It is unlikely that the United States will ever commit to such a massive and naïve project of social re-engineering of the type attempted in Vietnam, Iraq, and Afghanistan again in the future. At least we can hope so.

In countries where **nation**-building, as distinct from **state**-building, was not necessary, due to pre-existing national identities reinforced by common languages, religions, and ethnicities (Germany, Japan, and South Korea, for example), 70 years of continuous U.S. alliance and military presence backed by defense treaties and economic investment were demonstrably sufficient. All three of these countries were already nations—they were already "nation-built." U.S. forces are now based in these three countries, with the arguable exception of South Korea, as much for power projection in support of U.S. global interests as they are for ensuring domestic tranquility and deterrence of external aggression.

It is true that in Vietnam, Iraq, and Afghanistan, U.S. military forces in the field succeeded in temporarily halting enemy efforts to destabilize the countries, despite huge handicaps imposed on the U.S. military in each case by the political parameters of a limited war. But as North Vietnamese Colonel Tu apocryphally said to Colonel Harry Summers in Hanoi in 1972, that is also irrelevant.[84] In each case, there was no pervading sense in the armies of South Vietnam, Iraq, and Afghanistan of belonging to a nation and having a legitimate government worth fighting and, if necessary, dying for. In each case, the enemy did. As McNamara notes, "our misjudgments of friend and foe alike reflected our profound ignorance of the history, culture, and politics of the people in the area."[85] Or, as Secretary of Defense Ashton Carter admitted of the Iraqi Army in May 2015, "We can give them training, we can give them equipment; we obviously can't give them the will to fight."[85a]

## THE FUTURE OF AFGHANISTAN BY YEAR FROM 2015 TO 2019

The unanimous assessment of the intelligence community as released to the public in unclassified form is that the various elements of the Taliban have zero interest in a negotiated settlement, or even in negotiations beyond accepting the Afghan government's surrender. There is no possibility of a negotiated settlement. None. The exchange of the Taliban military high command for the suspected deserter Bowe Bergdahl in May 2014 had less to do with the return of Bergdahl than it did with a phantasmagorical desire on the part of the Office of the President's Special Representative to Afghanistan and Pakistan (SRAP) to prove that negotiations with the Taliban were possible as an imaginary stepping stone to peace talks. In order to achieve the *Mullahs'* specific short-term agenda, the Taliban simply gamed the Pollyannaish American negotiators who were over-eager to have "proof of concept" at any cost.[86] It was the equivalent of the Union in 1862 swapping Robert E. Lee, Stonewall Jackson, James Longstreet, J. E. B. Stuart, and Nathan Bedford Forrest for a Union private who wandered away from his post. The Taliban will continue to fight well beyond the departure of the United States by January 1, 2017. U.S. airpower, now directed by U.S. SFs and special operations forces (SOF) on the ground, will continue to disrupt massed conventional Taliban attacks on ANA outposts in the Pashtun areas of Afghanistan in those places where they are deployed, and for as long as it is available.

Some readers may be put off by the certainty of the following projection, but the point of this book has been, from the outset, that this outcome is, in fact, not difficult to predict using sound military strategic analysis, the kind of operational understanding taught at all Command and General Staff colleges, empirical tactical data, and the simple guidelines this analysis contains. Given this information, the mathematical level of probability of this projection is close to 100 percent. Here, therefore, is a year-by-year projection of what is going to happen in Afghanistan from 2015 to 2019, although the exact timing of specific tactical events may be off by some months on either side due to battlefield variables and the "fog of war."

**2015.**

Because of President Obama's recent order to extend U.S. air support to the ANA, 2015 will be largely a repeat of 2014, a period of slow decay and heavy casualties for the ANA and ANP, accompanied by incremental and modest improvements in ANA logistical capability. The Taliban will continue to achieve regular tactical success with hit-and-run attacks, inflicting casualties and seizing weapons, ammunition, and equipment as they did consistently in 2014. Operational success in the form of taking and holding several contiguous outlying districts is likely. Overrunning a remote provincial capital with a small government garrison, such as Parun, is possible. However, strategic success, defined here as taking and holding an entire province, and announcing the return of the Islamic Emirate of Afghanistan (IEA), is unlikely.

**2016.**

Assuming U.S. air support ends in December 2015 as is currently planned, Taliban gains in the south and southwest will be significant in 2016. Operational success is certain; strategic success is likely. Helmand province, in particular, is vulnerable without air support; a repeat in 2016 of the Taliban's campaign against Sangin district in the summer of 2014 would be successful without close air support (CAS). Seizure of Lashkar Gah will be more difficult for the Taliban, as urban warfare substantially favors the defender and is best suited to the ANA's sedentary nature. But ANA and ANP attrition will increase as momentum continues to shift to the Taliban. With attrition from the 215 Corps already running near 70 percent in 2014, the 215 Corps may simply disintegrate as four entire Iraqi divisions did at Mosul. Politically, the "unity government" established by rivals Ashraf Ghani and Abdullah Abdullah will either unravel completely or, at best, be dysfunctional, further destabilizing the situation.[87] If President Ghani pushes ahead with wholesale removal of officials and officers he believes to be corrupt in 2015, as he did on December 28, 2014, in firing more than 30 senior officials in Herat, including 15 district police chiefs,[88] major civil unrest in Kabul, Kandahar, Herat, and Mazar-i-Sharif is probable in 2016. Ousted warlords and power brokers may well incite their followers to violent protest. This will further distract and disaffect the security forces, some of whom will be tempted to take sides or consider the option of a coup, as happened during the election impasse in August 2014.[89] Iranian military support in the form of weapons and money to the Hazaras in the Hazarajat region will pose a diplomatic challenge for the United States similar to the situation in Iraq today.

**2017.**

As currently planned, December 31, 2016, will mark the departure of all foreign troops and support from Afghanistan, beyond a robust Office of Defence Assistance group in the U.S. Embassy. After that, the almost entirely Tajik ANA's position in the south and east will be militarily untenable. Surrounded by a countryside effectively owned by the Taliban; crippled by desertions; and unable to communicate, resupply, or reinforce, the garrisons of the 215th ANA Corps will collapse. The Taliban will achieve strategic success, as defined for this book. Helmand, Zabul, Uruzgan, Nimruz, Ghazni, and perhaps Wardak provinces will fall to the Taliban. Taliban leadership will announce the return of the IEA to Afghanistan. With the exception of parts of Kandahar province and Kandahar itself, the ANA 205 Corps will also collapse in the south. Barring assassination, however, the formidable Chief of Police of Kandahar Province Lieutenant General Abdul Raziq will be hard to dislodge.[90] The extent to which this can be controlled as an orderly strategic withdrawal, preserving portions of the 215 and 205 Corps to fight again, as opposed to complete disintegration (as was seen with the Iraqi Army in 2014), will be critical to establishing a stable defensive line and de facto partition.

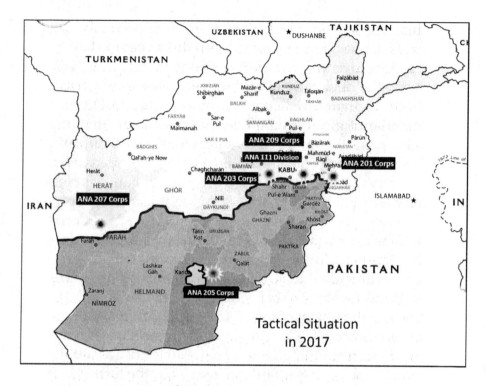

**Map II-1. Tactical Situation in 2017.**

The front will be a rough west-east line north of the Helmand River valley and eastwards to the Hindu Kush. Control of Kabul, with its symbolic importance as the capital city, will be contested. The current Taliban build-up in Wardak and Kapisa provinces in 2014 attests to the Taliban's intent to capture the city, and the almost daily attacks in Kabul in November 2014 may be seen as probes testing the city's defenses. Fighting in Wardak to keep the Taliban out of rocket and artillery range of Kabul will be intense. The CIA will have extensive evidence of Pakistani Army support to the Taliban inside Afghanistan, and one of the first challenges for the next U.S. President taking office in January 2017 will be deciding how to deal with this provocation. The United States will belatedly address this security crisis, and, as it did a year too late in Iraq due to misplaced faith in the Iraqi Army, the U.S. security policy apparatus will be forced into a crisis mode again to decide how to return to support the remainder of the ANA, and determine who in Afghanistan could be our Afghan equivalent of the Kurdish *Peshmerga*.[91]

## 2018.

The establishment of a de facto partition between Taliban-held Pashto-speaking Afghanistan and government-held Uzbek- and Dari-speaking northern Afghanistan will depend to a significant degree on the speed of the return of U.S. CAS and the extent of the presence of U.S. forward air controllers (FACs) in the form of SF/SOF teams inserted with those elements of the ANA still considered to be reliable. A very similar situation pertains in Iraq today. The ANA commando battalions are a leading candidate, as they are the best the Afghans have got. The Hazaras are another possibility. However, the Tajik, Uzbek, and Hazara remainder of the ANA will now be fighting on their own territory, defending their own homes and families, and their resistance will stiffen as it did from 1996 to 2000. Evacuation of the U.S. embassy and the embassy annex by air from Kabul to Mazar-i-Sharif is likely, as the fighting will be close to Kabul. There will be helicopters on the embassy roof again. Other regional players, including Iran[92] and Tajikistan,[93] have already expressed deep concern over the prospects of a Taliban government on their borders again and may intervene in the form of substantial military aid to northern armed groups.

**2019.**

The primary issue in 2019 will be who controls Kabul. Expeditionary U.S. air support operating from Shindand and Bagram air bases will be spread much thinner than is the case in Iraq today because of Afghanistan's far greater size, and sorties from an aircraft carrier in the Indian Ocean will have to traverse either Iranian or Pakistani airspace, with consequently shorter loiter times on station. As a result, there will be a greater reliance on drones.

Taliban territorial control in the south and east, however, now becomes a strategic liability for them, as it forces Taliban leadership to return from exile in Karachi, Peshawar, and Quetta or become irrelevant. This now exposes them to punishing U.S. air strikes. When they are no longer in densely populated Pakistani cities and closely guarded by the ISI, they can be targeted. This is the potential game-changer to induce the Taliban to accept "half a loaf" and agree to a bifurcated state. As a result of the U.S. ability to target and kill senior Taliban leadership for the first time when they return to Afghan soil, a *quid pro quo* may become possible in which the Taliban agree to establish their state capital in their spiritual capital city, Kandahar, which houses the sacred Cloak of the Prophet, and to leave Kabul to the north. Pakistan may consider half of Afghanistan sufficient strategic depth, although some scholars believe Pakistan's fear of the old dream of a Pashtunistan will drive Pakistani resistance to partition, as it could be a precursor to a Pashtun national independence movement.

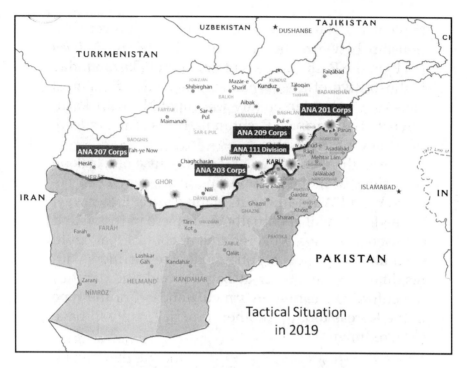

**Map II-2. Tactical Situation in 2019.**

Realistically, however, in a sound analysis, there is very little chance of a serious revival of the *Khudai Khidmatgar* (Red Shirt) Pashtunistan movement.[94] The level of political support for the Awami Workers' Party (AWP) in Pakistan, let alone for the more nationalistic offshoot *Pakhtunkhwa Milli Awami Party*, compared to the religious and political power of the Taliban is negligible. In the 2002 elections, the AWP received only 11.1 percent of the votes for the National Assembly and 9.4 percent of the votes for the Provincial Assembly.[95] In 2013, in the general elections, it declined still further, receiving only 5 percent of the vote in Khyber Pakhtunkhwa.[96] In 2015, the AWP has only six of the 99 regular seats in the Khyber Pakhtunkhwa Assembly.[97] This is not the stuff of a mass popular movement. The *realpolitik* of the relative power relationship between the AWP and the *Tehrik-i-Taliban* (TTP) in the Pashtun areas of northern Pakistan today is illustrative of this dynamic. The *Deobandi* Islamist construct is fundamentally incompatible with Pashtun nationalism and a Pashtun nation — as are, indeed, the Pashtuns themselves.

If not, the war will go on and, because of a lack on both sides of mobile supporting arms, may even become World War I-like in its static nature. Either way, the end state will eventually be de facto partition and a ceasefire along a brokered line of control that could eventually become a negotiated de jure partition, with residual U.S. air power at Bagram and Shindand as the enforcer, creating an armed stand-off of the type in the Koreas today. Another imperial map will have to be redrawn.

## ENDNOTES - PART II

1. "US Defense Chief: Iraqis 'Showed No Will to Fight ISIS in Ramadi'," ABC News, May 24, 2015, available from *abcnews. go.com/Politics/us-defense-chief-iraqis-showed-fight-isis-ramadi/ story?id=31273453.*

2. "Country Joe and the Fish," *The Well*, available from *www. well.com/~cjfish/game.htm.*

3. George Veith, *Black April: The Fall of South Vietnam, 1973-75*, New York: Encounter Books, 2013.

4. Ken Hughes, "The Myth That Congress Cut Off Funding for South Vietnam," History News Network, Washington, DC, The George Mason University, April 28, 2010, available from *historynewsnetwork.org/article/126150.*

5. *Ibid.*

6. "Raising an Army: Ten Rules," *War on the Rocks*, July 14, 2014, available from *warontherocks.com/2014/07/raising-an-army-ten-rules/#_.*

7. John Lewis, *Nothing Less Than Victory*, Princeton, NJ: Princeton University Press, 2101, p. 3.

8. Carl von Clausewitz, *On War*. London, UK: Penguin Books, 1982, pp. 251-252.

9. John Cook, *Afghanistan: The Perfect Failure*, Bloomington, IN: XLIBRIS: 2012.

10. Lardner, Richard, (Associated Press), "Investigation: Afghan Troops Ran, Hid During Deadly Battle," *Norfolk Virginian-Pilot*, June 11, 2011.

11. "Two Vets Who Deployed to Mosul Iraq," *Reddit*. Entry by "lostkeysblameHofmann," available *www.reddit.com/r/IAmA/comments/2gk0kh/i_we_are_two_vets_who_deployed_to_mosul_iraq_matt/.*

12. "Afghan Soldiers Ran, Hid during Attack," *The Boston Globe*, June 11, 2011, available from *www.boston.com/news/world/asia/articles/2011/06/11/afghan_soldiers_ran_hid_during_attack_us_report_says/?camp=pm.*

13. Doug Beattie, *An Ordinary Soldier*, London, UK: Pocket Books, 2009.

14. Mike Martin, *An Intimate War: An Oral History of the Helmand Conflict 1978-2012*, London, UK: C. Hurst & Co Publishers Ltd, 2014.

15. "After Push in Marja, Marines Try to Win Trust," *The New York Times*, February 28, 2010, available from *www.nytimes.com/2010/03/01/world/asia/01marja.html?pagewanted=all.*

16. "Clueless and Stoned: How US Forces See Their Local Comrades," *The London Times*, October 5, 2010, available from *www.thetimes.co.uk/tto/news/world/asia/afghanistan/article2752743.ece.*

17. "NATO "Mission Complete" in Afghanistan," *Nine Line*, January 9, 2015, available from *www.ninelineapparel.com/nine-line-news/nato-mission-complete-in-afghanistan/*.

18. *Ibid.*

19. "Get Out," *petrblt*, November 3, 2010, available from *https://petrblt.wordpress.com/2010/11/03/get-out/*.

20. "Green Berets Reveal Afghan National Army Soldiers' Incompetence: Reports Say ANA Troops Hide from Battle, Can't Lead or Fight at Night," *Washington Times*, October 26, 2014, available from *www.washingtontimes.com/news/2014/oct/26/green-berets-tell-of-afghan-national-army-soldiers/?page=all*.

21. SFC Keith Norris, U.S. Army, " The Afghan National Army: Has Capacity Building become Culture Building?" *Military Review*, November-December 2012, p. 32.

22. "Afghan Army Struggles in District Under Siege," *The New York Times*, September 11, 2013, available from *www.nytimes.com/2013/09/12/world/asia/afghan-army-struggles-in-district-under-siege.html?pagewanted=all&_r=0*.

23. Antonio Giustozzi, "The Afghan National Army: Sustainability Challenges Beyond Financial Aspects," Kabul, Afghanistan: Afghan Research and Evaluation Unit, February 2014, p. 1.

24. "Green Berets Reveal Afghan National Army Soldiers' Incompetence."

25. "Taliban Mount Major Assault in Afghanistan," *The New York Times*, June 27, 2014, available from *www.nytimes.com/2014/06/28/world/asia/taliban-mount-major-assault-in-afghanistan.html*.

26. *Ibid.*

27. "Being Led From Behind," *The Economist*, October 1, 2014, available from *www.economist.com/blogs/banyan/2014/10/afghanistans-army*.

28. "Taliban Overrun an Afghan Army Base," *The New York Times*, November 29, 2014.

29. Bing West, *A Million Steps*, New York: Random House, 2014.

30. *Ibid.*

31. Eric Bergerud, *The Dynamics Of Defeat: The Vietnam War In Hau Nghia Province*, Boulder, Co: Westview Press, 1993, p. 303.

32. Robert McNamara, *In Retrospect: The Tragedy and Lessons of Vietnam*, New York: Vintage Books, 1996, p. 322.

33. "NATO Report Says Taliban Captives Are Confident of Victory," *The Los Angeles Times*, February 1, 2012, available from *latimesblogs.latimes.com/world_now/2012/02/nato-report-says-taliban-captives-are-confident-of-victory.html*.

34. "Open Hearing: Current and Projected National Security Threats to the United States," U.S. Senate Select Committee on Intelligence, January 31, 2012, available from *www.intelligence.senate.gov/hearings/open-hearing-current-and-projected-national-security-threats-united-states-0#hrg*.

35. "Green Berets Reveal Afghan National Army Soldiers' Incompetence."

36. Arnold Isaacs, *Without Honor: Defeat in Vietnam and Cambodia*, Baltimore, MD: John Hopkins Press, 1998.

37. Available from *www.cnn.com/2010/WORLD/asiapcf/11/23/us.afghanistan.taliban/*.

38. "Iraq Army's Ability to Fight Raises Worries," *The Wall Street Journal*, June 22, 2014, available from *online.wsj.com/articles/iraq-armys-ability-to-fight-raises-worries-1403484149*.

39. *Ibid.*

40. McNamara, pp. 996, 322, 333.

41. Karl "Max" Weber, *Politik als Beruf* (*Politics as a Vocation*), Leipzig, Germany: Duncker & Humblot, 1926.

42. *Ibid.*

43. Morris Bishop, *The Middle Ages*, New York: Mariner Books, 2001.

44. "ISIS Jihadis Lure Arab Youths to Fight against Western Forces," *Pittsburgh Tribune-Review*, October 11, 2014, available from *triblive.com/usworld/betsyhiel/6948198-74/isis-says-abu#axzz3L LjUaGYZ*.

45. "A Tale of the Mullah and Muhammad's Amazing Cloak," *International New York Times*, December 19, 2001, available from *www.nytimes.com/2001/12/19/international/asia/19CLOA.html*.

46. Stewart Gordon, ed., *Robes of Honour: Khilat in Pre-Colonial and Colonial India*, Oxford, UK: Oxford University Press, 2003.

47. Andrew Petersen, *Dictionary of Islamic Architecture*, New York: Routledge, 1996, p. 120.

48. "International Peacebuilding: An Analysis of Peacemaking in Afghanistan," *Atlantic-Community.org*, May 21, 2010, available from *www.atlantic-community.org/app/webroot/files/articlepdf/International%20Intervention,%20an%20Analysis%20of%20Bonn%20Political%20Settlement%20in%20Afghanistan.pdf*.

49. History Learning Site, available from *www.historylearning-site.co.uk/douglas_macarthur.htm*.

50. John Dower, "The Showa Emperor and Japan's Postwar Imperial Democracy," Japan Policy Research Institute (JPRI) Working Paper No. 61, Cardif, CA: JPRI, October 1999, available from *www.jpri.org/publications/workingpapers/wp61.html*.

51. "No Ordinary Homecoming," BBC News, April 17, 2002, available from *news.bbc.co.uk/2/hi/south_asia/1936041.stm*.

52. *Ibid.*

53. "Afghanistan Needs A Hero: How A Unifying National Leader Can Bring Peace," *Huffington Post*, June 14, 2010, available from *www.huffingtonpost.com/michael-hughes/afghanistan-needs-a-hero_b_610622.html*.

54. Thomas Johnson and Chris Mason, "Refighting the Last War: Afghanistan and the Vietnam Template," *Military Review*, November-December 2009, Endnote 11, p. 14, available from *usacac.army.mil/CAC2/MilitaryReview/Archives/English/Military Review_20091231_art004.pdf*.

55. Selig Harrison, "Afghanistan's Tyranny of the Minority," *The New York Times*, August 16, 2009, available from *www.nytimes.com/2009/08/17/opinion/17harrison.html?_r=0*.

56. "Afghan Council Postponed, King Steps Aside," United Press International, June 10, 2002, available from *www.upi.com/Business_News/Security-Industry/2002/06/10/Afghan-council-post-poned-king-steps-aside/UPI-62001023745673/*.

57. "Afghanistan in 2013: A Survey of the Afghan People," Washington, DC: The Asia Foundation, 2013, available from *asiafoundation.org/country/afghanistan/2013-poll.php*.

58. Bryan Carroll and David A. Anderson, "Afghanistan Governed by a Federal System with Autonomous Regions: A Path to Success?" *The Long War Journal*, 2009, p. 29.

59. Paul Pillar, "Afghanistan Election Crisis: "Likely Fraud on a Million-Vote Scale Is a Big Gap to Bridge," *The National Interest*, July 20, 2014, available from *nationalinterest.org/blog/paul-pillar/afghanistan-political-culture-strikes-again-10847*.

60. "Public Lecture and Open Discussion, 'The Afghan National Army: Sustainability Challenges beyond Financial Aspects'," *ARU*, Tuesday, November 18, 2014, Kabul, Afghanistan: Afghanistan Research and Evaluation Unit, p. 5.

61. Bergerud, p. 3.

62. Jeffrey Record, "How America's Own Military Performance in Vietnam Aided and Abetted the 'North's Victory',"

Marc Jason Gilbert, ed., *Why the North Won the Vietnam War*, New York: Palgrave, 2002, p. 119.

63. McNamara, pp. 322, 333.

64. Ronald Spector, *Advice and Support: The Early Years, 1941-1960*, Stockton, CA: University Press of the Pacific, 2005, p. 379.

65. See, for example: Karl Wolfgang Deutsch, William J. Folt, eds., *Nation Building in Comparative Contexts*, New York: Atherton, 1966.

66. Carolyn Stephenson, "Nation Building," *Beyond Intractability*, January 2005, available from *www.beyondintractability.org/essay/nation-building*.

67. Paul Beinart, *The Good Fight: Why Liberals, and Only Liberals, Can Win the War on Terror*, New York: HarperCollins Publishers, 2006, p. 198.

68. James Dobbins, "Nation-Building: the Inescapable Responsibility of the World's Only Superpower," Santa Monica, CA: RAND Review, Summer 2003.

69. Godfrey Mwakikagile, *Statecraft and Nation Building in Africa: A Post-colonial Study*, Dar es Salaam, Tanzania: New Africa Press, 2014, p. 14.

70. Max Weber, "Politics as a Vocation," Hedwig Gerth and Freya Mills, eds., *From Max Weber: Essays in Sociology*, New York: Oxford University Press, 1946. p. 48.

71. "Suffering in Afghanistan Hits Record High—for Any Country," Gallup World Poll, December 5, 2014, available from *www.gallup.com/poll/179897/suffering-afghanistan-hits-global-record-high.aspx*.

72. *Ibid.*

73. "U.S. Aid to Afghanistan Exceeds Marshall Plan in Costs, not Results," *The Los Angeles Times*, July 31, 2014, available from *www.latimes.com/world/afghanistan-pakistan/la-fg-afghanistan-us-aid-outlook-20140731-story.html*.

74. Spending in July 2014 reached $104 billion dollars, and the population of Afghanistan in 2014 is approximately 31 million people: $104 billion divided by 31 million = $3.350.00.

75. "Afghanistan: Triumph or failure?" *The Daily Journalist*, January 3, 2015, available from *thedailyjournalist.com/elcafe/afghanistan-triumph-or-failure/*.

76. "SIGAR: Pentagon's Economic Development in Afghanistan 'Accomplished Nothing'," *Defense News*, November 18, 2014, available from *www.defensenews.com/article/20141118/DEFREG03/311180053/SIGAR-Pentagon-s-Economic-Development-Afghanistan-Accomplished-Nothing-*.

77. "Korean War Armistice Agreement," *FindLaw*, July 27, 1953, available from *news.findlaw.com/cnn/docs/korea/kwarmagr072753.html*.

78. Clay Blair, *The Forgotten War: America in Korea, 1950-1953*, New York: Times Books, 1987.

79. Richard Allen, *Korea's Syngman Rhee: An Unauthorized Portrait*. North Clarendon, VT: Charles E. Tuttle, 1960.

80. *Ibid.*

81. Kendall Gott, *Security Assistance: U.S. and International Historical Perspectives*, Fort Leavenworth, KS: Combat Studies Institute Press, 2006, p. 178.

82. Jeffrey Clark, *Advise and Support, the Final Years 1965-1973*, Washington, DC: Center of Military History, U.S. Army, 1988, p. 521.

83. "Hagel: Vietnam War's lessons still echo today," *Military Times*, January 22, 2015, available from *www.militarytimes.com/story/military/pentagon/2015/01/22/hagel-interview/22161401/*.

84. Richard Halloran, "Strategic Communication," *Parameters*, Carlisle PA: The Strategic Studies Institute and The U.S. Army War College Press, Autumn, 2007, p. 4.

85. McNamara, p. 322.

85a. "US Defense Chief: Iraqis 'Showed No Will to Fight ISIS in Ramadi'."

86. "The Truth Behind the Bowe Bergdahl POW Prisoner Swap," *Newsweek*, June 3, 2014, available from *www.newsweek.com/ truth-behind-bowe-bergdahl-pow-prisoner-swap-253218?piano_t=1*.

> [T]here appears to be far more at stake here than the return of Bergdahl, and this also may be part of a three-dimensional diplomatic chess game. Their future has been important in negotiations between the Afghan government, the United States and the Taliban in resolving the conflict.

87. Chris Mason, "Fraud and Folly in Afghanistan," *Foreign Policy*, September 23, 2014, available from *www. google.com/url?sa=t&rct=j&q=&esrc=s&frm=1&source=web& cd=1&ved=0CB4QFjAA&url=http%3A%2F%2Fforeignpolicy. com%2F2014%2F09%2F23%2Ffraud-and-folly-in-afghanistan%2F& ei=ITyGVNWdB8mwggSC2YOQCA&usg=AFQjCNHrAdmQMyKF VO-RYYQV_bxiINb8ag&bvm=bv.80642063,d.eXY*.

88. "President Sacks 30 officials in Herat," Pajhwok News Agency, December 28, 2014, available from *www.pajhwok.com/ en/2014/12/27/ghani-herat-evaluate-security-governance*.

89. Matthew Rosenberg, "Amid Election Impasse, Calls in Afghanistan for an Interim Government," *The New York Times*, August 18, 2014, available from *www.nytimes.com/2014/08/19/world/ asia/amid-election-impasse-calls-in-afghanistan-for-an-interim-govern-ment.html?_r=0*. Rosenberg was declared *persona non grata* and deported for his story.

90. "Powerful Afghan Police Chief Puts Fear in Taliban and Their Enemies," *The New York Times*, November 8, 2014, available from *www.nytimes.com/2014/11/09/world/asia/powerful-afghan-police-chief-puts-fear-in-taliban-and-their-enemies-.html*.

91. Mason.

92. Sumitha Narayanan Kutty, "Iran's Continuing Interests in Afghanistan," *The Washington Quarterly*, June 2014, available from *elliott.gwu.edu/iran%E2%80%99s-continuing-interests-afghanistan*.

93. "ISAF Withdrawal from Afghanistan to Make Tajikistan Strengthen Border Security," *TASS*, October 15, 2014, available from *itar-tass.com/en/world/754567*.

94. Mohammad Raqib, "The Muslim Pashtun Movement of the Northwest Frontier of India, 1930-1934," Maria J. Stephan, ed., *Civilian Jihad: Nonviolent Struggle, Democratization, and Governance in the Middle East*, New York: Palgrave Macmillan, 2009, p. 112.

95. Andrew Wilder, "Elections 2002," Craig Baxter, ed., *Pakistan on the Brink: Politics, Economics, and Society*, Oxford, UK: Lexington Books, 2002, p. 121.

96. "Election 2013: A Right Wing Victory," *International Viewpoint*, May 20, 2103, available from *www.internationalviewpoint.org/spip.php?article2971*.

97. Government of Pakistan, Provincial Assembly of Khyber-Pakhtunkhwa, available from official website, *www.pakp.gov.pk/2013/*.

# PART III:

# THE STRATEGIC LESSONS UNLEARNED FROM VIETNAM, IRAQ, AND AFGHANISTAN

The great enemy of the truth is very often not the lie —
deliberate, contrived, and dishonest — but the myth —
persistent, persuasive and unrealistic.[1]

John F. Kennedy

## IMPEDIMENTS TO STRATEGIC JUDGMENT

Neck deep in the Big Muddy, and the big fool said to
push on.[2]

Pete Seeger

Controlling the message in warfare is as old as
warfare itself. At Baghdad, in 1401, Tamerlane had
his warriors build a tower of 90,000 severed heads to
assist the city's population in assessing the pros and
cons of resistance or surrender.[3] Expressions of confidence in victory are a part of war, whether they are
called public affairs, strategic messaging, psychological operations, information warfare or propaganda,
in the old, more positive, pre-Nazi connotation of the
word.[4] One would hardly have expected International
Security Assistance Force (ISAF) commanders to say
publicly "the Afghan National Army is terrible" when
the audience included the Afghan National Army
(ANA), the enemy, and Afghan civilians. This American foreign policy by messaging is deliberate, simplistic, repetitive, and pervasive. For the withdrawal from
Afghanistan, in 2010 administration message crafters

came up with a year-by-year public "narrative." As Jack Fairweather notes:

> a U.S. PowerPoint presentation laid out what the West hoped would be the 'Key Tenets of the Afghan Narrative:' '2011/12, Notice what is different; 2012/13, Change has begun; 2013/14, Growing confidence; 2015, A new chance, a new beginning'.[5]

Reviewing the media reporting on Afghanistan since 2011, one can clearly see administration officials sticking to these talking points and repeating them in unison.

The danger to which civilian and military leaders alike are increasingly prone, however, is coming to believe in their own public messaging as if it were actually true, and making decisions based on it as if it were reality and not wishful thinking about how we would like the world to be. This optimism afflicted ISAF officers in general and National Military Training Center-Afghanistan (NMTC-A) officers in particular.[6] For a decade, notes a senior Afghan analyst, "whenever a problem with the ANA was raised, the typical response of NMTC-A was that 'we have a plan to solve that completely, so that isn't a problem anymore'."[7] A problem was no longer a problem if a staff officer had developed a plan to fix it, accompanied, naturally, by more positive messaging.

A corollary danger lies in the natural human desire to report success up the chain of command, and to design or modify metrics in a way that appears to support positive momentum. The author of this book attended many Afghan Interagency Operations Group (AIOG) meetings at which considerable pressure was applied and arguments made to upgrade unpleasant "yellow" (not so good) boxes on the color-coded "Progress Metrics" chart to "green" (good), to indicate up the chain of command that progress was assuredly being made. This, too, is a venerable aspect of warfare. When faced with the unhappy task of reporting an unbroken series of defeats to the Chinese Emperor in the 19th century, Mandarin officials arrived upon the solution of simply describing them all as victories.[8] A similar approach was taken in Vietnam, where "body counts" were notoriously inflated, and the daily Pentagon reports of battlefield success were dubbed the "Five o' Clock Follies" by a press corps no longer finding them credible.[9] Briefings on Afghanistan sometimes seem to emulate both the Mandarin and the Five o' Clock Follies solutions. As Anthony Cordesman notes:

> Since June 2010, the unclassified reporting the U.S. does provide has steadily shrunk in content, effectively 'spinning' the road to victory by eliminating content that illustrates the full scale of the challenges ahead. They also . . . were driven by political decisions to ignore or understate Taliban and insurgent gains from 2002 to 2009, to ignore the problems caused by weak and corrupt Afghan governance, to understate the risks posed by sanctuaries in Pakistan, and to 'spin' the value of tactical ISAF victories while ignoring the steady growth of Taliban influence and control.[10]

The Afghan Ministry of Defense (MOD) press office has copied the art. The frequent press statements from the Afghan MOD in Kabul exaggerating the number of Taliban killed in operations are known locally to the few foreign journalists still covering the war as the "Panj o' Clock Follies," using the Dari word for "five."[11] The war by messaging in English is also going strong, using the "Key Tenets of the Afghan Narrative" message plan adopted by the administration, with "Growing confidence" the message theme for 2014.[12] In a briefing on December 2, 2014, for example, ISAF spokesman Lieutenant Commander Justin Hadley told reporters "the Afghan National Security Forces are becoming more capable and stronger each day."[13] As has been shown, statistics indicate that just the opposite is true.

More recently, the outgoing commander of ISAF, Lieutenant General Joseph Anderson, said he was confident the Afghan police and army could prevent the Taliban from regaining territory next year. "This country is safer and more prosperous than ever," he said. "The insurgents have been beaten back and the Afghan National Security Forces are carrying the fight to the enemy."[14] In fact, no part of this statement is statistically true: The country is not safer than ever: Taliban attacks and Afghan civilian deaths both reached a new record high in 2014, according to the United Nations.[15] The country is not more prosperous than ever: Afghanistan not only remained the poorest country in the world despite reconstruction spending which has surpassed the Marshall Plan, it also set a historical record in 2014 for the most human suffering in modern world history.[16] Absolute poverty has risen by about 10 percentage points in Afghanistan since the beginning of the war. Life expectancy has fallen to 44 years, and infant mortality has increased to reach 150 per thousand.[17] The Afghan economy is shriveling.[18] The insurgents have not been "beaten back," (a somewhat disingenuous statement in itself, as one must wonder, if they have never been winning, why were they being "beaten back"?) the Taliban now control more territory than ever.[19] And the security forces are not carrying the fight to the enemy: they are more sedentary, less mobile, and conducting fewer patrols and offensive operations than ever before.[20] As Phillip Münch of the *Afghan Analysts Network* noted in January 2015:

> Observers frequently describe the Afghan National Security Forces (ANSF) as rather passive and defensive, with the usually better paid and supplied special forces often being the only forces who regularly take offensive action.[21]

After 13 years and a trillion dollars spent,[22] security is so bad in the capital city that the flag-furling ceremony for Operation ENDURING FREEDOM had to be held in secret at an undisclosed location in Kabul out of concern that the ceremony would be attacked by the Taliban.[23] The main roads in the capital are so unsafe that "[North Atlantic Treaty Organization] forces often fly by helicopter over the 5-10 [kilometers] from the coalition headquarters to the capital's military airport because of the threat of suicide bombers on the roads."[24]

Again, the reasons for this public position are obvious, but this approach carries with it the corollary danger that Americans and Afghans alike will, in fact, believe all is well, and Afghans in particular will not be moved to the sense of urgency and the kind of national mobilization necessary at this point to combat the Taliban. Noting this kind of danger, a January 2011 report by the Afghan Nongovernmental Organization (NGO) Security Office in Kabul advised foreigners working in Afghanistan that its assessment of the security situation was:

> sharply divergent from [ISAF] 'strategic communication' messages suggesting improvements. We encourage [nongovernment organization personnel] to recognize that no matter how authoritative the source

of any such claim, messages of this nature are solely intended to influence American and European public opinion ahead of the withdrawal, and are not intended to offer an accurate portrayal of the situation for those who live and work here.[25]

In fact, such "strategic messaging" generally befuddles both our Afghan allies and our enemies in Pakistan.[26] Coming from a completely different culture in which not dissembling and politeness rank equally high, Afghan civilians and most senior officers outside the press office are often baffled why U.S generals would say things they know are not true. The Pakistanis, on the other hand, ever fond of conspiracy theories,[27] ask of the ANA, "why has the U.S. sunk billions of dollars in a project that had no chance to deliver?"[28] One Inter Services Intelligence Directorate (ISI) theory is that, since much of the ANA training and infrastructure development was carried out by former American military personnel working as contractors, there was money to be made in the ANA training business.[29] The ISI and the Pakistani Army have other conspiracy theories about resources and dark U.S. intentions in Central Asia, but until recently, apparently, they did not consider the possibility that U.S. officers might actually believe what they were saying.[30] As former ISI Lieutenant General Asad Durrani put it:

> [until] recently I had believed that the U.S. was too smart not to know about the ANA's limits and was pumping it up as a ruse. But since an American friend of mine who is a keen observer of the Afghan scene is convinced that the ANA could carry out its mission with some help from its mentors, it is quite possible that Washington too has faith in this role.[31]

The same messaging was a constant feature of the war in Vietnam. Just as U.S. officials today are pointing to the escalating casualties suffered by the ANSF as proof of their fighting spirit, senior U.S. officials in Vietnam "cited the death of 'approximately ten thousand Vietnamese' through 1962 as proof of their willingness to prosecute the war."[32] Defeats like the Battle of Ap Bac were described as victories. Admiral Harry Felt (Commander in Chief Pacific [CINCPAC] from 1958 to 1964) told reporters in Saigon that Ap Bac "was a Vietnamese victory — not a defeat as the papers say."[33] As historian David Toczek notes:

> CINCPAC was not only sure of a [South] Vietnamese victory at Ap Bac, but he also believed in total victory, proclaiming that 'I am confident the Vietnamese are going to win their war.' Despite the 'recent casualties suffered by Vietnamese forces at Ap Bac,' the war in Vietnam [CINCPAC said] was 'taking a generally favorable course.'[34]

When American war correspondents reported on the Army of the Republic of Vietnam's (ARVN) "lack of aggressiveness," as is seen in the ANSF today, Commander US Military Assistance Command Vietnam (COMUSMACV) General Paul Harkins praised them and emphasized their casualties.[35] This positive messaging continued right up until the end of the war. On November 21, 1967, COMUSMACV General William Westmoreland told U.S. news reporters the United States was winning in Vietnam. "I am absolutely certain that whereas in 1965 the enemy was winning," Westmoreland said, "today he is certainly losing."[36] In 1970, as the United States was preparing to withdraw from Vietnam, President Richard Nixon told the American people that "progress in training and equipping South Vietnamese forces has substantially exceeded our original expectations last June. . . . Very significant advances have also been made in pacification."[37]

The same optimism of messaging seen in Afghanistan and Vietnam also pervaded the creation of the Iraqi Army as well. In 2006, the *Armed Forces Journal* reported that "in fighting spirit, small-unit tactics and discipline, the fledgling Iraqi army has made substantial progress."[38] In testimony before the House Armed Service Committee in January 2008, Commander of the Multi-National Security Transition Command-Iraq, Lieutenant General James Dubik, stated:

> The Iraqis are proud of what they are accomplishing. They are proud of themselves, and they are committed to their own success. And we are meeting with some success, Mr. Chairman. The Iraqi Security Forces are bigger and better than they have been at any time since the effort to establish them began. I attribute this to three things . . . the rejection of Al Qaeda and other extremists by much of the Iraqi population. More people want to serve. More people feel invested in their own futures . . . we have seen significant growth across the board. We are seeing the Iraqi's want to take more responsibility for the battlespace . . . It is money well spent. [39]

Six months later, Dubik told Congress, "There has been huge progress. There has been significant improvement in every possible way you can measure it" and reported the Iraqi Army would be proficient to take over its own security in 2009.[40] In May 2008, Anthony Cordesman at the Center for Strategic and International Studies (CSIS) stressed the "need to recognize that very real progress is being made."[41] Late in 2009, U.S. Army Colonel Fred Kienle, an Iraqi Army trainer, gushed that:

> They're all soldiers. What we find is, particularly the Iraqi soldiers are patriots. They are risking their lives to be soldiers, as most soldiers do, but them particularly . . . they see a new Iraq. They're committed to what they're doing.[42]

In fact, none of this messaging reflected reality, but so deeply had this positive public messaging pervaded the public sphere, and so convinced were military leaders by it, that many were shocked when the Iraqi Army collapsed in 2014. Jessica Lewis, a former Army intelligence officer and the director of research at the Institute for the Study of War, said, for example, "the fact that the four ISF [Iraqi Security Forces] northern divisions were overrun or collapsed with almost no resistance is extraordinary, and hugely alarming."[43] "The U.S. military worked incredibly hard in the 2005-08 time frame to build the ISF into a professional, national force that represented all Iraqis," echoed retired Lieutenant General David Barno, "and the fact that . . . [it] folded so fast when confronted with Islamic extremists is a very dangerous development."[44] Company and field grade officers with closer knowledge of the U.S. effort in Iraq and less exposure to the talking points, however, were not taken by surprise. "They weren't soldiers because they wanted to be soldiers," explained Marine First Lieutenant Dave Jackson, who fought with Iraqi forces during his two deployments to Iraq. "They were soldiers because they wanted a job."[45] A Marine colonel, who asked to remain anonymous because he is on active duty, said that after their own families, the soldiers and leaders were loyal to their tribes and then their religion. "Iraq as a nation falls at the bottom of the list. Combine this with lack of cohesion, unity, loyalty, and camaraderie among themselves, and you have an organization that will disintegrate under pressure."[46] The fact that Iraq is not a nation, and never has been, and the fact that there was in reality nothing in Baghdad that the men of the Iraqi Army were going to fight and die for, made this outcome entirely predictable. It was a strategic repetition of South Vietnam.

What causes the disconnect between rational intelligence assessments made by seasoned intelligence professionals and the optimistic positions of military officers? In some cases, it is a result of confirmation bias, the remarkable psychological phenomenon in which many people, when presented with facts that show their positions and views to be completely wrong, actually **reinforce** their wrong beliefs rather than changing them.[47] Another factor is bureaucratic "groupthink" — the tendency of people involved in a decision to try to sense which way a decision is shaping up and then make sure to be on board and stay on board with the eventual decision. The author observed this as a major factor in foreign policymaking in the interagency on Afghanistan from the middle levels up. Groupthink is defined as occurring:

> when a desire for conformity within a group transcends rational thought and issues of right and wrong. When this happens, individuals in a group fail to express their doubts about the group's dynamic, direction or decisions because of a desire to maintain consensus or conformity. Thus the group may be on a headlong rush to error or disaster and no-one speaks up because they don't want to rock the boat. Groupthink can affect communities of any size from small groups to whole nations.[48]

In other words, savvy bureaucrats and politicians can sense which way a decision is taking shape and often feel compelled to be on the "winning side" of the policy argument. Dissent is not career-enhancing. Individuals, too, can be affected by what is known as the "blind spot bias" — the inability of persons to see confirmation bias and groupthink within themselves.

Another danger is bureaucratic path dependency. Path dependency is defined as a state of organizational inertia and the historical imprinting of decisionmaking by which organizations lose their flexibility and become inert or even locked in.[49] Experts in organizational dynamics say this happens in three phases. Phase I, the "Preformation Phase," is characterized by a broad scope of action. In Phase II, the "Formation Phase," a dominant action pattern emerges "which renders the whole process more and more irreversible." Choices and options narrow, and "it becomes progressively difficult to reverse the . . . initial pattern of action." Phase III, the "Lock-in Phase," occurs when the dominant decision pattern becomes fixed and gains a deterministic character; eventually, the actions are fully bound to a path. One particular choice or action pattern has become the predominant mode, and flexibility has been lost. Even new entrants into this field of action cannot refrain from adopting it. U.S. Government policy is particularly vulnerable to this process.[50] Capturing this dynamic in 1983, historian Arnold Isaacs summarized the reasons for failure in Vietnam in his history of the final years of the war as follows:

> Misperceiving both its enemy and its ally, and imprisoned in the myopic conviction that sheer military force could somehow overcome adverse political circumstances, Washington stumbled from one failure to the next in the continuing delusion that success was

always just ahead. This ignorance and false hope were mated, in successive administrations, with bureaucratic circumstances that inhibited admission of error and made it always seem safer to keep repeating the same mistakes, rather than risk the unknown perils of a different policy.[51]

The intellectual habits of thought of military institutions also tend to become predictable and calcified. The same thing has occurred in Afghanistan today. As Afzal Amin notes:

> . . . the personality type (in psychological terms) favored across NATO in terms of recruitment, training, promotion and retention is the linear-thinking process-focused maintainer of the status quo, which was ideal for holding back the Soviets while keeping our force readiness at optimum levels. We didn't want mavericks and non-conformists so we didn't have them. But for the wicked problems that were Iraq and Afghanistan, mavericks were precisely what we needed, the problem-solvers and the independent thinkers. Recognizing our own limitations is both wise and necessary. We must learn from the institutional failure to gain victory in Afghanistan if we are to have any hope that the escalating crises in Iraq and Syria are to be resolved any time soon.[52]

## GUIDELINES FOR FUTURE WARS

He was impregnably armored by his good intentions and his ignorance.[53]

> Graham Greene, of Alden Pyle, the idealistic Central Intelligence Agency (CIA) agent in his novel, *The Quiet American*

What should elected leaders, civilian officials, and military officers consider when future military intervention is proposed? First, nation-building is impossible, except perhaps in the negative sense: if you invade a country, you may unite them in temporary opposition to you and foster a more nationalistic identity. But the Afghans have united to eject a lot of invaders over the last 2,000 years and it has not made them a nation. Be wary of collaborators telling you what you want to hear. In any coercive environment, there will always be the Chalabis, al Malikis, Karzais, Khalilzads, Kys, and Thieus on the weaker side ready to collaborate with the stronger, but usually only for their own personal self-aggrandizement.[54] Before seriously considering military intervention (as opposed to humanitarian relief, for example) in a foreign country that will require the extended presence of U.S. troops (for example, longer than 90 days), the best academic experts in the United States should be summoned to provide an assessment of the extent to which the people of that country have a developed sense of nationhood. If a country has not reached a point where nation-building is no longer necessary, conventional military intervention involving occupation should be off the table, because failure in that environment is inevitable, as Vietnam, Iraq, and Afghanistan clearly prove. Successful state-building cannot occur until a country has reached the "nation-built" stage of development, and nation-building cannot be done by any foreign country. It is, by definition, a slow, evolutionary, internal social process.

Second, state-building is possible, but it is best done by civilians, and it takes between 70 and 100 years to go from poverty, illiteracy, and economic under-development to a liberal democracy with stable economic growth. The role of the military is to defend it, not to build it. Germany, Japan, and Korea are proof of this. The nations of Central Europe and Eastern Europe have undoubtedly benefited greatly in terms of political and economic progress by their membership in NATO, the presence of small numbers of NATO forces, and the guarantee of security provided by Article 5. In no case in Central or Eastern Europe, however, was nation-building necessary, and a steady and reliable influx of Western support, including trade and defense commitments, provided a jump start on post-communist state-building. The Ukraine, on the other hand, was clearly not "nation-built." The key in such cases would be understanding the lengthy time span of military commitment required, the nature of that commitment, and the degree to which the people of the country in question would support a long-term U.S. military peacekeeping presence. Not all nations are pro-American.

Third, peacekeeping is possible, but coercive peace-creating in a failed state is not. The U.S. interventions in Somalia and Lebanon come to mind. An international peacekeeping presence could work, for example, in a post-Castro Cuba. No nation-building would be required—Cubans have a strong sense of being Cuban. American troops might be represented along with those of Cuba's Latin neighbors—Cubans have no great dislike for the United States,[55] despite 60 years of a misguided economic embargo.[56] The political turmoil that inevitably follows the collapse of communism in a country with no democratic history could be stabilized by an international military presence that prevents the vacuum from being filled by undemocratic opportunists in the army or police forces or by wealthy carpetbaggers from Florida. Such a stability presence could allow a legitimate indigenous process to develop democratic tendencies over a period of several decades. This is not to advocate such a policy, merely to provide a real world example of a nation where state-building, backed by extended military peacekeeping, could assist a nation in transition if properly considered and planned, and all the necessary conditions pre-exist (i.e., a permissive environment, a receptive population, a functioning justice system, reasonable literacy levels, and a strong sense of nationhood). Needless to say, however, the assistance in building civil institutions should be done by civilians, not the military.

Finally, what do these lessons from South Vietnam, Iraq, and Afghanistan say about the future role of the U.S. Army and the U.S. military? What larger overall lessons should be learned from Germany, Japan, and Korea—and Vietnam, Iraq, and Afghanistan? What missions should the U.S. military of the future be prepared to carry out? The answer is primarily two-fold: First is the ability to conduct long-term peacekeeping operations, such as the one in South Korea, which require a substantial, benign military presence in barracks ready to go to war against an aggressor literally at a moment's notice with intense lethality—"to fight," as the current expression has it, "outnumbered and win."

The second function is essentially expeditionary: To be able to go into a country where events have dramatically threatened American citizens and/or Americans interests, strike a military target hard in a way that will change the balance of power in favor of moderate indigenous elements, and get back out within 90 days. Why? Because staying longer does not help where nationhood does not exist. Operation

DESERT STORM is a textbook example of this kind of intervention, but the U.S. Army will rarely have a year to prepare for a designer war and a carefully choreographed walkover in the future.

On the other hand, 8 years in Vietnam, 11 in Iraq, and 13 in Afghanistan did not change the outcome or made it worse. All were ill-considered, because none were nations. In each case, the adversaries of America's nation-creation illusion were and are stronger than the united will of the indigenous people to fight for it. Ho Chi Minh was more committed to a reunited Vietnam than he was to communism, as Office of Strategic Services (OSS) advisor Archimedes Patti, Foreign Service Officer Paul Kattenburg, and others reported.[57] Saddam Hussein was a horrible human being, but he kept the lid on Iraq's volcanic internal dynamics, kept Iran in check, and allowed no terrorists on his soil. Rural Afghanistan is a 14th century society that is several centuries at best from being a nation ready for state-building. It may never be. Bangladesh, East Timor, Eritrea, and South Sudan all exist today because a unified Pakistan, Indonesia, Ethiopia, and Sudan were never going to be nations within their existing colonial maps. It is heresy to the State Department,[58] which has always fought against it, but sometimes the best way to solve a problem is to draw a new map.

## CONCLUSIONS

U.S. foreign policy and military engagement in any part of the world should hinge first and foremost on the extent to which the country under consideration is a nation. The first corollary to this book might be that the greater the extent to which a country is a nation, the lesser the probability that U.S. military engagement will be ever considered or needed there, because instability can largely be graphed in parallel with nationhood. Many definitions have been offered by political scientists for the term "nation," but for the purposes of this book, the word will mean a country in which a broad majority of the people identify themselves at a national level. In other words, a country in which, when asked, the great majority of the people would answer the questions "Who are you?" and "Where are you from?" with the names of their countries: "Peru," for example, or "Switzerland," rather than by any more localized identities, such as clan, tribe, ethnicity, religion, or linguistic group.

This is, of course, a very superficial definition; the concept of nationhood and identity are complex and fluid. The sense of national identity should not be conflated with pride in nationality; these are quite different. However, for the purposes of discussion, it provides a readily understandable and easily established baseline on which to plot a country's social and political development. It is the kind of litmus test that anyone can apply and, if answered objectively and honestly, casts the country in question into clear focus. Indeed, it could easily be plotted on a linear graph.

In Vietnam, the CIA planned and carried out a coup in 1963, which inadvertently resulted in the assassination of South Vietnamese President Ngô Đình Diem and his brother.[59] This was followed by a prolonged period of coups and instability. In Afghanistan in 2001, the United States invaded to remove the Taliban from power, then subverted the will of the Afghan people, prevented the Afghan King Zahir Shah from returning to the throne in a ceremonial role as a symbol of national unity to confer legitimacy on the state, and refused the Taliban's offer of surrender.[60] Because Plan A, Abdul Haq, was betrayed to the Taliban by the ISI and killed in 2001,[61] an Afghan political nonentity named Hamid Karzai was placed in power instead because he was the only other Afghan the CIA had on its payroll.[62] In Iraq, the United States invaded in 2003 to remove Saddam Hussein from power and have him hanged after a fair trial. (Hussein's defense attorney noted that "this court is a creature of the U.S. military occupation, and the Iraqi court is just a tool and rubber stamp of the invaders."[63] As *The Washington Post* observed, "Americans have drafted most of the statutes under which Hussein and his associates are being tried."[64] Amnesty International called the trial "deeply flawed and unfair."[65]) The U.S. Government then conspired to install Nouri al-Maliki as the Prime Minister of Iraq.

None of these deliberately planned foreign policies of regime change and armed nation-creation during civil wars (Vietnam and Afghanistan) or in barely contained civil wars (Iraq) worked out well. (To these three could be added the U.S. intervention in a civil war in Somalia in 1992, the U.S. intervention in a civil war in Lebanon in 1983, and the U.S. overthrow of the nationalist leader Mohammad Mossadegh in Iran in 1954 to put the Shah in power.) Diem was unpopular but his successors were worse, and their corruption and incompetence fueled the Viet Cong insurgency. Hamid Karzai turned out to be a corrupt, incompetent, and mentally unstable milquetoast, and his failure to even try to reign in his kleptocracy and reduce opium production, from which his own family made billions of dollars,[66] aided the rise of the many tentacles of the Taliban comeback. In Iraq, Nouri al-Maliki took none of the steps required to build trust and a sense of inclusion among Iraq's religious factions, especially the majority Sunni Muslims, and instead concentrated power among his own Shia minority,[67] giving rise, first, to a Sunni insurgency that claimed the lives of thousands of American Soldiers, and ultimately to the radical Sunni terrorist group, Islamic State in Iraq and Syria (ISIS). In all four cases of deliberate U.S. regime change by force and installing our man in power in Asia in the past 50 years (including Iran), the results have been catastrophically and diametrically opposed to those intended.

In Vietnam, Iraq, and Afghanistan, there were American experts who advised, or would have advised if they had been consulted, against all of these courses of action. Yet, in most cases, the Americans who knew these countries best were either not spoken to, not heeded, or deliberately excluded from the room at the time these fateful decisions were being made. In the case of Vietnam, Patti, for example, knew Ho Chi Minh well, having fought with him against the Japanese in Vietnam during World War II. Patti advised that Ho could be one of our most important post-war allies in Asia, and his commitment to communism was skin deep.[68] As Patti later recalled:

> In my opinion the Vietnam War was a great waste. There was no need for it to happen in the first place. At all. None whatsoever. During all the years of the Vietnam War no one ever approached me to find out what had happened in 1945 or in '44. In all the years that I spent in the Pentagon, Department of State, in the White House, never was I approached by anyone in authority. However, I did prepare a large number, and I mean about, oh, well over fifteen position papers on our position in Vietnam. But I never knew what happened to them. Those things just disappeared, they just went down the dry well.[69]

Paul Kattenburg was another unheeded Vietnam expert. Kattenburg served in Vietnam in the late-1950s and early-1960s and knew the country as well as any American alive. On August 31, 1963, Kattenburg dissented at a meeting of senior Kennedy administration officials which prepared the ground for sending in U.S. combat troops, including Chairman of the Joint Chiefs of Staff General Maxwell Taylor, Secretary of State Dean Rusk, National Security Adviser McGeorge Bundy, and the President's brother and Attorney General Robert Kennedy. Kattenburg told them the expanded U.S. war would fail, the South Vietnamese were already tired of the war, and that Diem was secretly negotiating with the north. Kattenburg later wrote, "[T]here was not a single person there that knew what he was talking about."[70] Taylor, who wanted a war in Vietnam, challenged him, while Rusk derided Kattenburg's statement as "speculative."[71] Bundy knew Kattenburg was telling the truth because he had received a very similar report from his trusted aide, Michael Forrestal, just weeks before, but said nothing.[72] Kattenburg was never invited to another policy meeting.[73]

How, one wonders, is this possible? In a nation populated with the world's leading experts on most foreign countries, how can critical foreign policy decisions be made that often deliberately exclude those experts who do not agree with the proposed policy? The answer is, sadly, that the policymakers do not want them there. In the case of Vietnam, for example, outgoing U.S. Ambassador to Saigon Frederick Nolting argued in late-August 1963 against a coup. Few Americans knew Vietnam better than Nolting.[74] He, too, was ignored. The disregard for the advice of experts on Vietnam was subsequently borne out by former Secretary of Defense and chief architect of the Vietnam War Robert McNamara. In 1993, McNamara addressed the Council on Foreign Relations in New York. As Bruce Nussbaum notes, McNamara told the audience:

> he had made a mistake. The protesters had been right all along. The war was unwinnable from the start. The domino theory was ridiculous. Nationalism had been confused with communism. There had never been a serious threat to U.S. security.[75]

When an audience member asked McNamara why he did not listen to the experts, "McNamara smiled down from the podium and said: '. . . they weren't in our circle'."[76]

There also were, and are still today, tightly closed "circles" for the wars in Iraq and Afghanistan. The list of military and government civilian experts opposed to the Iraq War was extraordinarily long and deep.[77] Again, an administration determined to have a war was not interested in the views of American experts who warned that Saddam Hussein was not a nice man, but he was sitting on the lid to Pandora's Box and keeping Iran in check, and that removing him would destabilize the entire region. In regard to Afghanistan, days after the terrorist attacks of September 11, 2001, American-born Middle East journalist Eric Margolis wrote a piece entitled "Spare Afghanistan from U.S. 'Nation-Building'" in the *Toronto Sun*:

> In all my years as a foreign affairs writer, I have never seen a case where so many Washington 'experts' have all the answers to a country that only a handful of Americans know anything about. President George Bush, who before election could not name the presi-

dent of Pakistan, now intends to redraw the political map of strategic Afghanistan, an act that will cause shock waves across South and Central Asia. Anyone who knows anything about Afghans knows . . . they will never accept any regime imposed by outsiders. . . . Washington's plan for 'nation-building' in Afghanistan is a recipe for disaster that will produce an enlarged civil war that draws in outside powers.[78]

Other American experts and Foreign Service Officers counseled against the notion of nation-creation in Afghanistan and the administration's approach. While serving as the representative of the Bureau of Political Military Affairs (PM) to the ad hoc Afghan policy group in 2001 and to the Afghan Interagency Operations Group (AIOG) thereafter, for example, the author wrote a Briefing Memo in November 2001 to James Dobbins strongly urging that King Zahir Shah be returned to Kabul in a largely ceremonial role and laid out the reasons why. It was neither answered nor heeded. Dobbins had never been to Afghanistan and knew nothing about the country, but he and his inner coterie knew better.[79]

These "circles" are not naturally occurring phenomena. Politicians, bureaucrats, and generals make them. Agreement with the policy is generally the criteria for admission to the circle. Groupthink rules. Once inside the circle, groupthink is compounded by the kind of "participant compliance" found by experts like Dr. Muller Weitzenhoffer in stage hypnosis carnival acts, wherein members are compliant because of the social pressure felt in the environment constructed in the briefing room.[80]

The most disturbing interpretation of Vietnam, Iraq, and Afghanistan is that senior leaders had already formed a consensus of what they wanted to do in a given foreign policy situation to fit it into a larg-er, overarching ideology, and were not interested in contrary views and advice. It is well-documented, for example, that then-Secretary of Defense McNamara wanted a war in Vietnam and deliberately withheld critical information about the second (nonexistent) at-tack in the Gulf of Tonkin on August 4, 1964.[81] It is also a well-known and well-documented part of the his-tory of the run-up to the invasion of Iraq that within 48 hours of the attacks of September 11, 2001, then-Secretary of Defense Donald Rumsfeld instructed his intelligence analysts to "find a connection to Iraq."[82] Another unlearned strategic lesson of Vietnam, Iraq, and Afghanistan is the need to open the "circles." Indeed, perhaps law should require it in order to in-crease transparency, give American civilian experts from outside of government a greater opportunity to provide advice and counsel, and counterbalance ad-ministration war hawks. The genetic inbreeding of foreign policy seldom ends well.

The U.S. military has influence over all of these po-tential pitfalls in deciding foreign policy. Perhaps more so than is the case in any other mature democracy, the U.S. military is itself included in the formulation of policy. In most democracies, foreign policy is crafted by civilian elements of a nation's foreign ministry in consultation with elected leadership, and, if a solution to a problem is believed to involve military operations, the military leadership of that country is then called in and tasked with carrying out the intent of govern-ment. In the United States, senior military leadership is involved in policymaking from the beginning. This, perhaps not surprisingly, has resulted in the foreign policy of the United States arriving at military solu-tions more often than is the case with most of our democratic allies around the world. Whether or not it is the result of the military-industrial complex that President Dwight Eisenhower warned the American people about, the U.S. Government prioritizes war over peace. There are more military personnel playing in military bands today for military parades than there are State Department diplomats in total around the world trying to prevent conflict.[83]

But as a result of this greater engagement in policymaking, the U.S. military is poised, almost uniquely among our friends in the world, to be able to push back against all of the potential systemic flaws in decisionmaking that involve the use of military force. If the State Department, the National Security Council, and the CIA are not consulting outside academic experts, the Department of Defense certainly can. In a political system in which the military is not simply given a tasking but in fact helps craft the tasking, it has considerable bureaucratic leverage in the final product. One must ask: Why was the U.S. military willing, even eager, to rush into Vietnam, Afghanistan, and Iraq with ground troops and carry out complex military operations in those countries without inviting top experts into the room who would have said, "No, you **really** don't want to do that"? Real leadership means surrounding yourself with people who will tell you your plan is bad, not sycophants eager to tell you it is great. In the end, if all else fails, as retired Marine officer Frank Hoffmann suggests, "When civilian policy masters will not establish the necessary conditions for strategic success, military officers can retire, resign, or request reassignment."[84]

When the problem is a military one, the confidence, aggressive spirit, and determination to find a way to win embodied by American military and naval officers are the qualities that make the United States a deadly foe in battle. When the problem is political, however, they can become an impediment to strategic vision. American military and naval officers are taught from their first day in training to take care of the men and women under their command and not to squander their lives. In total, 65,069 American Soldiers, Sailors, Airmen, and Marines lie dead from the wars in Vietnam, Iraq, and Afghanistan, all of which were predictable and predicted strategic failures. As this book has shown, they are all dead because the "circle," as McNamara termed it, was closed, experts were deliberately excluded from policymaking because they did not concur with prevailing groupthink, and senior officers went along for the ride to do their best with the mission they were given. The most outspoken critics of America's military, like Lieutenant General Herbert McMaster,[85] retired Colonel Andrew Bacevich,[86] and former Marine Lieutenant Colonel Frank Hoffman, have criticized the military establishment, or the officer corps, for not standing up to civilian leaders, for being too willing to try to get the job done, or for being, in Hoffman's harsh words, "yes men."[87] Some extreme critics have even gone as far as suggesting that America is becoming a new Sparta, where endless wars give professional officers a chance to prove their skills and reach higher rank.[88]

The correct courses of action—leaving Diem in power and helping him find an acceptable path to reunification, possibly under a "one country, two systems" approach of the type used in Hong Kong, for example; allowing Afghanistan's king to return to the throne as 75 percent of the country demanded, and then allowing the Afghans to sort out their own government; and leaving Saddam Hussein in power as an unsavory alternative to obviously far worse potential futures—were, in fact, all recommended by experts in each case before these decisions were implemented. The cost in blood and national treasure resulting from not listening to them is almost incalculable. At the end of the day, each of these tragedies was the result of an almost willful overreach of national power in countries which were not and are not yet nations. What historian George Herring wrote of Vietnam could stand as the epitaph of all three interventions: "an enduring testament to the pitfalls of interventionism and the limits of power."[89] The lessons for senior military officers are clear, but the question remains: will they be learned **this** time?

## ENDNOTES - PART III

1. Speech given for the Yale University commencement on June 11, 1962, Charlottesville, VA, University of Virginia Miller Center, available from *millercenter.org/president/speeches/speech-3370.*

2. Victor Wallis, "Song and Vision in the U.S. Labor Movement," Eunice Rojas and Lindsay Michie, eds., *Sounds of Resistance: The Role of Music in Multicultural Activism*, Vol. 2, Santa Barbara, CA: ABC-CLIO, LLC, 2013, p. 55.

3. William D. Rubinstein, *Genocide,* New York: Routledge, 2014, p. 28.

4. E.g., information or ideas that are spread by an organized group or government to influence people's opinions.

5. "Afghanistan: Coming to the Bad End of the Good War," *War on the Rocks*, Washington, DC, December 16, 2014, available from *warontherocks.com/2014/12/afghanistan-coming-to-the-bad-end-of-the-good-war/?singlepage=1.*

6. "ISAF Officer Brushes Off Increased Afghan Death Toll," *Trans Radio News Service*, March 20, 2013, available from *www. talkradionews.com/pentagon/2013/03/20/afghan-security-transition-update.html#.VJX1DAFABg*.

7. Interview with author, November 12, 2014.

8. Beatrice Bartlett, conference paper "Opening Up the Archives," New Haven, CT: Radcliffe Institute, Harvard University, p. 8, available from *isites.harvard.edu/fs/docs/icb.topic98010.files/bbartlett.pdf*.

9. "The Press: Farewell to the Follies," *Time*, February 12, 1973, available from *content.time.com/time/magazine/article/0,9171, 903831,00.html*.

10. Anthony Cordesman, *Afghanistan and the Uncertain Metrics of Progress: Part One: The US Failures That Shaped Today's War*, Washington, DC: Center for Strategic and International Studies (CSIS), February 22, 2011, available from *csis.org/publication/afghanistan-and-uncertain-metrics-progress-part-one-us-failures-shaped-todays-war*.

11. Author's conversation with a foreign journalist in Kabul, Afghanistan, December 6, 2014.

12. "Afghanistan: Coming to the Bad End of the Good War."

13. "Afghanistan's Heavily Guarded Capital No Longer Immune from Violence," *Stars and Stripes*, December 2, 2014, available from *www.stripes.com/news/afghanistan-s-heavily-guarded-capital-no-longer-immune-from-violence-1.316436*.

14. "Five killed in Afghanistan as Taliban Storm Kandahar Police Station," *Reuters*, December 8, 2014, available from *www. reuters.com/article/2014/12/08/us-afghanistan-attack-idUSKBN0J-M1AE20141208*.

15. "Civilian Deaths in Afghanistan Reach New High in 2014: UN," *World Post*, in conjunction with the *Huffington Post*, December 20, 2014, available from *www.huffingtonpost.com/2014/12/19/civilian-deaths-afghanistan_n_6355856.html*.

16. "Suffering in Afghanistan Hits Record High—for Any Country," *Gallup World Poll*, December 5, 2014, available from *www.gallup.com/poll/179897/suffering-afghanistan-hits-global-record-high.aspx*.

17. "Afghanistan: Triumph or failure?" *The Daily Journalist*, January 3, 2015, available from *thedailyjournalist.com/elcafe/afghanistan-triumph-or-failure/*.

18. "Worsening Security in Afghanistan," *Express Tribune*, December 15, 2014, available from *tribune.com.pk/story/806721/worsening-security-in-afghanistan/*.

19. "Taliban Making Military Gains in Afghanistan," *The New York Times*, July 26, 2014, available from *www.nytimes.com/2014/07/27/world/asia/taliban-making-military-gains-in-afghanistan.html*.

20. "Green Berets Reveal Afghan National Army Soldiers' Incompetence: Reports Say ANA Troops Hide From Battle, Can't Lead or Fight at Night," *The Washington Times*, October 26, 2014, available from *www.washingtontimes.com/news/2014/oct/26/green-berets-tell-of-afghan-national-army-soldiers/?page=all*.

21. Phillip Münch, "Operation Resolute Support," *Afghan Analysts Network*, p. 7, available from *https://www.afghanistan-analysts.org/wp-content/uploads/2015/01/20150112-PMuench-Resolute_Support_Light.pdf*.

22. "How the War in Afghanistan Went So Wrong," *The London Evening Standard*, January 8, 2014, available from *www.standard.co.uk/lifestyle/books/how-the-war-in-afghanistan-went-so-wrong-9965733.html*.

23. "One Sentence that Shows How Badly America Failed in Afghanistan," *Vox*, December 29, 2014, available from *www.vox.com/2014/12/29/7464111/afghanistan-war-failure*.

24. "Smaller NATO Mission Has Big Job to Train Afghan Army in Time," *Reuters*, January 6, 2015.

25. "Truth, Lies and Afghanistan," *Armed Forces Journal*, February 1, 2012, available from *www.armedforcesjournal.com/truth-lies-and-afghanistan/*.

26. See Carlotta Gall, *The Wrong Enemy*, New York: Houghton-Mifflin, 2014.

27. "Pakistanis Love Conspiracy Theories," *Deutsche Welle*, October 16, 2012, available from *www.dw.de/pakistanis-love-conspiracy-theories/a-16307473*.

28. Musa Khan Jalalzai, *Whose Army? Afghanistan's Future and the Blueprint for Civil War*, New York: Algora Publishing, 2014, Foreward.

29. *Ibid.*

30. *Ibid.*

31. *Ibid.*

32. David Toczek, *The Battle of Ap Bac, Vietnam: They Did Everything But Learn from It.* Monterey, CA: Naval Institute Press, 2007, p. 123.

33. *Ibid.*

34. *Ibid.*

35. *Ibid.*

36. General William Westmoreland statement to the press, November 21, 1967, *The History Channel*, available from *www.history.com/this-day-in-history/westmoreland-tells-media-the-communists-are-losing*.

37. "Presidential Statement: Nixon's Televised Vietnam Speech," *CQ Almanac* Archives, available from *library.cqpress.com/cqalmanac/document.php?id=cqal70-1290853*.

38. "Building an Iraqi Army," *Armed Forces Journal*, January 1, 2006, available from *www.armedforcesjournal.com/building-an-iraqi-army/*.

39. "Statement of Lieutenant General James Dubik, U.S. Army, Commander Multi-National Security Transition Command—Iraq on Iraqi Security Forces January 17, 2008," available from *www.loc.gov/resource/lcwa00010250.7uxr4YUdhYeHL xxEyPYgBw/#?time=20090902070721&url=armedservices.house. gov%2Fpdfs%2FFC011708%2FDubik_Testimony011708.pdf.*

40. "Iraqi Forces Estimated to Become Proficient in '09," *USA Today*, July 9, 2009, available from *usatoday30.usatoday.com/news/ washington/2008-07-08-3418976217_x.htm.*

41. Anthony Cordesman, "Iraqi Force Development 2008," Washington DC: CSIS, 2008, available from *csis.org/files/media/csis/ pubs/080527_isf_report.pdf.*

42. "Iraqi and US Soldiers Build New Iraqi Army," *Voice of America*, October 29, 2009, available from *www.voanews.com/ content/a-13-2005-02-14-voa57-67523017/386980.html.*

43. "Understanding Iraq's Disappearing Security Forces," *The National Journal*, June 19, 2014, available from *www.national-journal.com/white-house/understanding-iraq-s-disappearing-security-forces-20140619.*

44. *Ibid.*

45. "Veterans Not Surprised Iraq's Army Collapsed," *Al Jazeera*, June 28, 2014, available from *america.aljazeera.com/watch/ shows/america-tonight/articles/2014/6/28/how-did-iraq-s-armycollaps-esoquickly.html.*

46. "The Iraqi Army Never Was," *The American Conservative*, October 9, 2014, available from *www.theamericanconservative.com/ articles/the-iraqi-army-never-was/.*

47. D. Ariely, *Predictably Irrational: The Hidden Forces that Shape Our Decisions*, New York: HarperCollins, 2008.

48. Definition of "groupthink," *The Rational Wiki*, available from *rationalwiki.org/wiki/Groupthink.*

49. Jörg Sydow and Georg Schreyögg, "Organizational Path Dependence: Opening the Black Box," *Academy of Management Review*, Vol. 34, No. 4, 2009, pp. 689–709.

50. *Ibid.*, pp. 691-692.

51. Arnold Isaacs, *Without Honor: Defeat in Vietnam and Cambodia*. Baltimore, MD: John Hopkins Press, 1998.

52. Afzal Amin, "In Afghanistan the West Suffered from Institutional Failure. Let's Learn from It," *The Guardian*, October 28, 2014.

53. Graham Green, *The Quiet American*, New York: Penguin Books, 1957, p. 163.

54. See, for example, Mikolaj Kunicki, "Unwanted Collaborators: Leon Kozłowski, Władysław Studnicki, and the Problem of Collaboration among the Polish Conservative Politicians in World War II," *European Review of History: Revue européenne d'histoire*, Vol. 8, Issue 2, 2001, pp. 203-220.

55. "Dispelling Four Misconceptions about Travel to Cuba," *The Huffington Post*, April 13, 2013, available from *www.huffingtonpost.com/peggy-goldman/traveling-to-cuba_b_3062395.html*.

56. "It's Time for the U.S. to End Its Senseless Embargo of Cuba," *Forbes Magazine*, January 16, 2013, available from *www.forbes.com/sites/realspin/2013/01/16/its-time-for-the-u-s-to-end-its-senseless-embargo-of-cuba/*.

57. Interview with Archimedes L. A. Patti, 1981, available from *openvault.wgbh.org/catalog/vietnam-bf3262-interview-with-archimedes-l-a-patti-1981*.

58. State Department opposed to creation of East Timor, see Noam Chomsky, "East Timor Retrospective," *Le Monde Diplomatique*, October, 1999, available from *www.chomsky.info/articles/199910--.htm*; State Department opposed to breakup of Yugoslavia, see Matjaž Klemenčič, "The International Community and the FRY/Belligerents," The Scholars' Initiative: Resolving the Yugoslav Controversies, Report of Research Team

5, West Lafayette, IN: Purdue University, p. 2, available from *www.cla.purdue.edu/history/facstaff/Ingrao/si/Team5Report.pdf*; State Department opposed to independence of Bangladesh: "Bangladesh War of Independence," *New World Encyclopedia*, available from *www.newworldencyclopedia.org/entry/Bangladesh_War_ of_Independence#USA_and_USSR*; State Department opposed to independence of South Sudan and Eritrea, Andrew S. Natsios, *Sudan, South Sudan, and Darfur: What Everyone Needs to Know*, Oxford, UK: Oxford University Press, 2012, available from *https:// books.google.com/books?id=3oS-815ScpcC&pg=PT66&lpg=PT66&dq =State+Department+was+opposed+to+independence+of+south+sudan &source=bl&ots=c0Gym9tk0x&sig=mJ3Fsv-8LsoO8sEKRIlL7DRJ8i0 &hl=en&sa=X&ei=fl6WVODhAsyrgwTLi4H4Aw&ved=0CGEQ6AE wCQ#v=onepage&q=State%20Department%20was%20opposed%20 to%20independence%20of%20south%20sudan&f=false*.

59. James W. Douglass, *JFK and the Unspeakable: Why He Died and Why It Matters*, New York: Simon and Schuster, 2010, p. 186.

60. Ahmed Rashid, *Descent into Chaos: The U.S. and the Disaster in Pakistan, Afghanistan, and Central Asia*, New York: Penguin Books, 2008.

61. "U.S. Looks for Someone to Trust," *The Village Voice*, October 30, 2001.

62. "Karzai Admits to Being on Secret US Payroll," *Russia Today* (RT), April 29, 2013, available from *rt.com/usa/afghanistan-cash-corruption-karzai-547/*.

63. "Saddam Verdict Date 'Rigged' for Bush," *The New Zealand Herald*, November 5, 2006, available from *www.nzherald.co.nz/ world/news/article.cfm?c_id=2&objectid=10409222*.

64. "Hussein Trial Halts Again, Setting Off Wave of Criticism," *The Washington Post*, January 25, 2006.

65. "Iraq: Amnesty International Deplores Death Sentences in Saddam Hussein Trial," *Amnesty International*, November 5, 2006.

66. "Karzai Family's Wealth 'Fuelling Insurgency," *The Independent* August 7, 2009, available from *www.telegraph.co.uk/news/worldnews/asia/afghanistan/5991447/Karzai-familys-wealth-fuelling-insurgency.html*.

67. "Iraq Crisis: Obama Makes It Clear—Caretaker Prime Minister Nouri al-Maliki Should Go," *The Independent,* August 11, 2014, available from *www.independent.co.uk/news/world/americas/iraq-crisis-obama-makes-it-clear--caretaker-pm-nouri-almaliki-should-go-9662909.html*.

68. Interview with Patti.

69. *Ibid.*

70. William Conrad Gibbons, *The U.S. Government and the Vietnam War: Executive and Legislative Roles and Relationships, Part II: 1961-1964,* Princeton, NJ: Princeton University Press, 2014, p. 161.

71. Bruce Nussbaum, "Marching America into a Quagmire," *Business Week,* November 30, 1998.

72. *Ibid.*

73. Paul Kattenburg, *The Vietnam Trauma in American Foreign Policy: 1945-75,* Piscataway, NJ: Transaction Publishers, January 1, 1980.

74. Frederick Nolting, *From Trust to Tragedy: The Political Memoirs of Frederick Nolting, Kennedy's Ambassador to Diem's Vietnam,* New York: Praeger, 1988.

75. Nussbaum.

76. *Ibid.*

77. On August 14, 2003, the *Boston Globe* reported that the CIA and the State Department's Bureau of Intelligence and Research (INR) had both assessed before the invasion of Iraq that "Iraqi society and history showed little evidence to support the creation of democratic institutions" as a result of Iraq's "history of repression and war; clan, tribal, and religious conflict."

In January 2003, the Strategic Studies Institute of the U.S. Army War College warned that "tensions among Iraqi religious, ethnic, and tribal communities" would make forming a post-invasion government difficult, warned of the dangers of "fragmentation," and expressly warned against disbanding the Iraqi army, described as "one of the few forces for unity within the country."

In the January/February 2004 issue of *The Atlantic Monthly*, James Fallows reported the CIA was opposed to a process like the Bonn conference in Iraq because "rivalries in Iraq were so deep, and the political culture so shallow, that a similarly quick transfer of sovereignty would only invite chaos." There were other early prominent voices who warned against the war and its consequences.

In 2002, Scott Ritter, a Nuclear Weapons Inspector in Iraq from 1991-98, argued against an invasion and expressed doubts about the George W. Bush administration's claims that Saddam Hussein had a weapons of mass destruction capability. Other leading public figures opposed the war, including Morton Halperin; Brent Scowcroft; former Chairman of the Joint Chiefs of Staff Hugh Shelton; retired Marine General Anthony Zinni; Ambassador Joseph Wilson (who exposed the faked yellowcake evidence); career diplomats like John Brady Kiesling, John Brown, and Mary Ann Wright; military leaders, including former Chairman of the Joint Chiefs of Staff William Crowe, former Director of the National Security Agency Lieutenant General William Odom, former Commander of U.S. forces in the Middle East Joseph Hoar, former Assistant Secretary of Defense for Special Operations H. Allen Holmes, former Ambassador to the United Nations Donald McHenry, and former Air Force Chief of Staff General Merrill McPeak. Other former government officials, including Jack Matlock, Jr., a member of the National Security Council under Ronald Reagan; former Ambassador to the Soviet Union John Reinhardt; former Director of the United States Information Agency Ronald I. Spiers; Under Secretary General of the United Nations for Political Affairs and a former Director of the CIA Stansfield Turner; and former chief counterterrorism adviser on the National Security Council for both the Bill Clinton and the George W. Bush administrations, Richard Clarke, argued that the invasion of Iraq would bolster the efforts of Islamic radicals who had long predicted that the United States planned to invade an oil-rich Middle Eastern country.

78. "Spare Afghanistan from U.S. 'Nation-Building'," *Toronto Sun*, September 30, 2001, available from *www.twf.org/News/Y2001/0930-SpareAfghan.html*.

79. Author's personal recollection.

80. Andre Weitzenhoffer, *The Practice of Hypnotism*, New York: John Wiley & Sons, Inc., 2000, pp. 400, 418-419.

81. Gareth Porter, "How LBJ Was Deceived on Gulf of Tonkin," *Consortium News*, April 5, 2014, available from *https://consortium-news.com/2014/08/05/how-lbj-was-deceived-on-gulf-of-tonkin/*.

82. "The Iraq War—Part I: The U.S. Prepares for Conflict, 2001," *The National Security Archive*, Washington, DC: The George Washington University, available from *www2.gwu.edu/~nsarchiv/NSAEBB/NSAEBB326/*.

83. "Vast Number of Military Bands May Not be Music to Gates's Ears," *The Washington Post*, August 24, 2010, available from *www.washingtonpost.com/wp-dyn/content/article/2010/08/23/AR2010082304711.html*.

84. Frank Hoffman, "Dereliction of Duty Redux?" Washington, DC: Foreign Policy Research Institute, November 2007, available from *www.fpri.org/articles/2007/11/dereliction-duty-redux*.

85. Herbert McMaster, *Dereliction of Duty: Lyndon Johnson, Robert McNamara, The Joint Chiefs of Staff, and the Lies that Led to Vietnam*, New York: Harper Perennial, 1997.

86. Andrew J. Bacevich, *Breach of Trust: How Americans Failed Their Soldiers and Their Country*, New York: Metropolitan Books, 2013.

87. Hoffman.

88. Jonah Goldberg, "Obama's Vision for a Spartan America," *National Review*, January 27, 2012, available from *www.national-review.com/articles/289402/obama-s-vision-spartan-america-jonah-goldberg*; Charlie Lewis, "A New Sparta: America's Threatening Civil-Military Gap," *Kennedy School Review*, Vol. 11, 2011, p. 170.

89. George Herring, *America's Longest War*, New York: Wiley, 1979, p. 358.

# APPENDIX I

## CENTRAL INTELLIGENCE AGENCY GUIDE TO THE ANALYSIS OF INSURGENCY

**Figure I-1. Title Page for the
Central Intelligence Agency Guide to the
Analysis of Insurgency.**

The following text is transcribed from the Central Intelligence Agency's (CIA) "Guide to the Analysis of Insurgency," a handbook intended to provide government analysts with a way of interpreting the progression of events on the ground when making intelligence assessments for the U.S. Government. The guide is unclassified and was released to the public many years ago. The CIA text is transcribed verbatim and is intersticed with observations (in italics) pertaining to the situation in Afghanistan in December 2014. Using these U.S. Government metrics and publicly available reportage, by any reasonable, objective assessment of the facts on the ground, the Taliban is in the "late stages of a successful insurgency."

Ability to protect supporters and local population:

- Do government forces adequately protect local supporters on a 24-hour basis?
*Afghanistan: No*
- Do national army "reaction forces" respond quickly and effectively to reports of guerrilla attacks on local civilian militias or pro-government communities?
*Afghanistan: Rarely, if ever.*
- Do government officials sleep in villages, or do they seek protection of armed camps?
*Afghanistan: Government officials never sleep outside district centers, it would be suicidal. Insurgent forces always sleep among the local population.*
- Are national army troops/guerrillas viewed locally as threatening outsiders or as helpful allies?
*Afghanistan: 50 percent of the Afghan population say they view the police with "some" or "a great deal of fear." The army is generally viewed positively. The Taliban overall has the support of approximately a third of the population, mostly in the south where the insurgency is most active.*

Local military effectiveness:

- Are local civilian militia aggressive in small unit, day and night patrolling, or do they avoid contact with the enemy?
*Afghanistan: Where they exist, local militias are defensive in nature. Patrolling is not done.*
- Do government/guerilla forces have an effective intelligence network at the local level?
*Afghanistan: This is difficult to assess. The effectiveness of both enemy and government intelligence networks may be roughly equal.*

- How disciplined are government/insurgent forces in combat? Do they usually recover the weapons and bodies of fallen comrades before retiring?

  *Afghanistan: Insurgent forces are highly disciplined. They rarely, if ever, leave weapons or casualties behind. Government police checkpoints are often wiped out to the last man. Government bodies are left behind, and are usually stripped of weapons and ammunition by the insurgents.*

- Are local government/insurgent forces capable of executing coordinated attacks against nearby enemy strongpoints?

  *Afghanistan: Insurgent forces routinely execute coordinated attacks against government strongpoints. There were more than 6,000 attacks in the last year. Government forces rarely, if ever, operate offensively and show little aggressive spirit.*

**Late-Stage Indicators of Successful Insurgencies.**

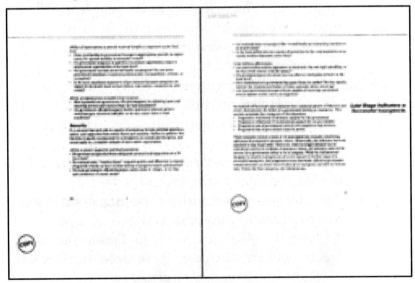

**Figure I-2. Late-Stage Indicators of Successful Insurgencies.**

An analysis of historical cases indicates that a common pattern of behavior and events characterizes the defeat of a government battling an insurgency. This pattern comprises four categories of developments:

- Progressive withdrawal of domestic support for the government.
- Progressive withdrawal of international support for the government.
- Progressive loss of government over population and territory.
- Progressive loss of government coercive power.

These categories include a total of 14 interrelated and mutually reinforcing indicators of prospective insurgent victory. Historically, the indicators have not appeared in any single order. Moreover, while no single indicator can be considered conclusive evidence of insurgent victory, all indicators need not be present for a government defeat to be in progress. While the indicators are designed to identify a progression of events typical of the final stages of a successful insurgency, this progression is not inevitable. Effective government countermeasures can block the evolution of an insurgency and shift its momentum. Within the four categories, the indicators are:

Progressive withdrawal of domestic support for the government:
- Withdrawal of support by specific, critical segments of the population:
  *Afghanistan: Much of the ethnic Pashtun segment of the population supports the insurgents. Very few of other ethnic group members do so.*

- Growing popular perception of regime illegitimacy:

  *Afghanistan: The regime has never had any legitimacy in the Weberian sense.*
- Popular perception of insurgents as leading nationalists:

  *Afghanistan: Not applicable. The insurgents are viewed by their fellow ethnic group members as waging a legitimate jihad.*
- Insurgent co-optation, incorporation, or elimination of other major opposition groups to the insurgency:

  *Afghanistan: No. Some militias have changed sides and some police have defected, but there have been no major defections of other elements of the counterinsurgents.*

Progressive withdrawal of international support for the government:
- Withdrawal of foreign support by specific, critical allies.

  *Afghanistan: The withdrawal of more than 90 percent of foreign troops from Afghanistan can only be interpreted as such.*
- Increasing international support for the insurgents.

  *Afghanistan: No. Only Pakistan continues to support the insurgents.*

Progressive loss of government over population and territory:
- Significant expansion of territory under insurgent control:

  *Afghanistan: Beyond any reasonable dispute.*

- Escalation of guerilla/terrorist violence:
  *Afghanistan: Beyond any reasonable dispute. Guerilla violence reached record levels in 2014.*
- Increasing inability of government to protect supporters/officials from attack:
  *Afghanistan: Beyond any reasonable dispute. Government casualties and attacks in the capital city reached record levels in 2014.*
- National economy increasingly weakened by insurgent violence:
  *Afghanistan: Beyond any reasonable dispute. The Afghan economy has been shrinking every year since 2011.*

Progressive loss of government coercive power:
- Military plots or coups against the government:
  *Afghanistan: No. The rumor of a coup was reported by the New York Times in 2014.*
- Armed guerilla forces multiplying in size:
  *Afghanistan: Beyond any reasonable dispute.*
- Lack of sufficient government troops for counterinsurgency:
  *Afghanistan: Beyond any reasonable dispute.*
- Government seriously negotiating sharing of power with rebels:
  *Afghanistan: The government would very much like to negotiate a power-sharing arrangement with the jihadis. In January 2015, President Ghani offered three cabinet ministries to the Taliban.[1] However, the Taliban are convinced of inevitable victory and are not interested in negotiations beyond the release of their prisoners.*

# ENDNOTES - APPENDIX I

1. "Taliban 'Reject Offer of Afghan Government Posts'," *BBC*, January 9, 2015, available from *www.bbc.com/news/world-asia-30737664.*

# APPENDIX II

## RELATIVE COMBAT POWER:
## WARGAMING BEYOND ONE-TO-ONE

Calculating military outcomes in Afghanistan is too often reduced to a simple 1:1 numerical ratio. For example, "there are 10,000 counterinsurgent troops and 2,500 insurgents," wherein these are thought of as interchangeable units of equal strength. However, this kind of reductionist representation of the situation is dangerous and highly misleading, because it completely omits any **qualitative** factors. No one would seriously suggest that 100 U.S. Army Rangers were the equal of 100 Afghan national policemen, for example. Yet, in most discussions of Afghan security, these forces would be routinely reduced to: "100" and "100."

To address this, some innovative wargames of the 1970s developed a way to build in quantifiable factors of mobility, range, power in attack, and tenacity in defense for different units. For example, the 101st Airborne at Bastogne would receive a high rating for defense. This would make it harder in the wargame to defeat that unit in an attack. Conversely, a 1945 German *Volksturm* unit comprised of boys and old men with outdated weapons might receive a defensive factor of zero, because the wartime experience of such last ditch units was that they did not put up much of a fight and had no tactical power. A World War II wargame in which a battalion of 101st Airborne soldiers was the same as a *Volksturm* battalion was unrealistic, and this innovation made it more realistic. To give another example, a *Waffen SS* division would be given a high attack rating because they were generally populated with fanatical, highly motivated, tactically skilled, well-trained, obedient and well-equipped fighters.

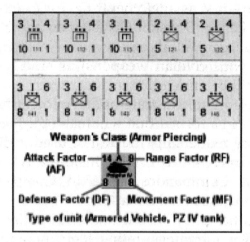

Examples of wargame counters, top, and an explanation of the factors represented as numbers in each of the four corners, bottom. The factors rate the unit shown in terms of its power in attack, power in defense, mobility, and the range of its weapons.

## Figure II-1. Examples of Wargame Counters and an Explanation of the Factors.

The same principle could be applied to Afghanistan today. A Navy SEAL team and a squad of Afghan National Police (ANP) might be the same number of men, but they should not be evaluated militarily on a 1:1 numerical equivalent basis in analyzing outcomes in Afghanistan. It would also be unrealistic, and it would not reflect battlefield realities. In the same way, in a broader sense, referring to the Afghan National Security Forces (ANSF) as a single unified number of men in uniform is equally misleading. The Afghan

National Army (ANA) is stronger militarily than the ANP, and agglomerating them as "128,500 ANSF" rather than "75,000 ANA and 53,500 ANP" is highly misleading—just as agglomerating, for example, one *Waffen SS Panzer* Division (20,000 men and 500 Tiger tanks) and three *Volksturm* divisions (30,000 old men and boys with civilian weapons) as simply "50,000 men" would be misleading in a wargame.

In an effort to illustrate and reinforce this point graphically in a format that will make the most sense to a military readership, the author used unclassified data from open sources to evaluate the ANA, ANP, ALP, ANA Commandos, an ANA Company reinforced by a U.S. Special Forces A Team, and a 100-man Taliban battle group in the same format introduced by the 1970s wargames, rating their mobility, range of firepower, and tenacity in offense and defense (i.e., combat power). Figure II-2 shows, purely for purposes of illustration, how the relative combat power and tactical factors might compare. Thus, the Taliban company counter could easily attack and overcome an ANP platoon counter, as they regularly do in real life, but could not successfully attack an ANA company reinforced by a U.S. Special Forces A Team, because its associated close air support is overwhelming in the defense rating—as is true in real life.

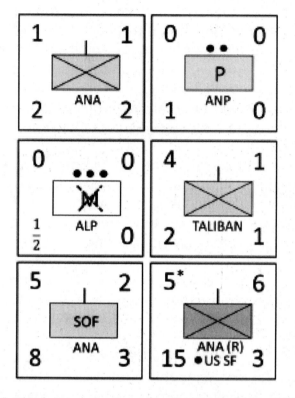

Notional game counters for the ANA, ANP, ALP, Taliban, ANA Commando, and an ANA company reinforced by a U.S. Special Forces A Team, to illustrate the differences in military tactical strength and combat value of the units. The asterisk indicates that U.S. forces no longer engage in offensive operations.

**Figure II-2. Notional Game Counters.**

The purpose of this Appendix is to attempt to add nuance to the analysis of the current security situation in Afghanistan by introducing qualitative thinking into a discussion that today is dominated by quantitative thinking.